The Words Unspoken

The Words Unspoken

The Hidden Power of Language

Debra C. Smith

Carolina Academic Press
Durham, North Carolina

Copyright © 2008
Debra C. Smith.
All Rights Reserved.

Library of Congress Cataloging-in-Publication Data

Smith, Debra C.
  The Words unspoken : the hidden power of language / by Debra C. Smith.
    p. cm.
  Includes bibliographical references and index.
  ISBN-13: 978-1-59460-174-3 (alk. paper)
  ISBN-10: 1-59460-174-7 (alk. paper)
  1. English language--Social aspects--United States. 2. English language--Spoken English--United States. 3. English language--Variation--United States. 4. Language and culture--United States. I. Title.

PE2808.8.S65 2007
427.973--dc22

2007016473

Carolina Academic Press
700 Kent Street
Durham, North Carolina 27701
Telephone (919) 489-7486
Fax (919) 493-5668
www.cap-press.com

Printed in the United States of America.

Cover design by Stephon Best, a graduate of
Northwest School of the Arts in Charlotte, North Carolina.

Contents

Acknowledgments	vii
Introduction	xi
Chapter One Language in Story	**3**
Cathy Carraway	52
Virginia Carraway	54
Becca Carraway	55
Belle Williams	55
Gerald Williams	57
Chapter Two Language in Television	**63**
Good Times (1974–1979)	64
The Fresh Prince of Bel-Air (1990–1996)	68
Chapter Three Language in Hip-Hop	**75**
The Secret Language of Jay-Z's 99 *Problems* and Kanye West's *Jesus Walks*	77
Chapter Four Language in Society	**95**
Appendix A: Survey	96
Chapter Five Language Possibilities in the Classroom	**103**
Teaching Slang, Hip-Hop and Idioms in the Classroom	109
Appendix C: Adapted from the Diversity Kit Education Alliance, Brown University	112
Bibliography	117
Index	123

Acknowledgments

I have always been intrigued by language. As a teen I sat before the television admiring the way words effortlessly rolled off the tongues of newscasters, dreaming that one day I myself might one day command an audience. And, like others, I have had my share of times of being misunderstood with regard to language. For instance, as a 15-year-old taking drivers' education class, I noticed a gap in communication between my white instructor and me. When "Coach Varney" would say "Okay, Debra, break her," I would speed up, incensing him. He often yelled at me, asking why I went faster when he was telling me to "brake." This went on for a week and I was truly close to failing the practical portion of driver's education. I had to train myself and my ear to actually slow down when Varney said "brake," as opposed to what I was accustomed to the word meaning which, was "break for it," or "break out" or simply hit the gas and go faster. This book captures my stories, my friends' stories and the stories of my students and others who have a narrative to tell about language.

While I admit to not being a linguist by training, my fascination for language is no less passionate. In this decade humans are intrigued by varieties of "language." Language isn't just "bodily" or spoken word. Just recently I played a cell phone company's signature ring tone for my students who could easily recognize it as "the Nokia ring." Southwest Airlines would lead us to believe that a computer tone sends prospective travelers running back to their desktops to check the latest flight sales, and the honking sound that interrupts your favorite television show "speaks" to us in such a way that we check the rolling words at the bottom of the television screen to determine if there is a nearby weather hazard. This project allowed me to explore all the "sounds" that have impacted my world and to examine the values and judgments we often place upon sounds. Research for this work reveals things about my family and friends that has pedagogic possibility. Moreover, it reveals personal stories about my family and friends. In that way, it was difficult to write at times because the memories that help to fill the pages carry with them a range of emotions—some still fresh enough to sting when they are questioned. For example, I left this portion of the manuscript laying out one day when my teenage niece and I were visiting together. As she chatted freely on the telephone for what seemed like an entire day, she picked up my manuscript which I had carelessly left out in the open and she read the first two sentences. "I can't believe you did this stuff!" she scoffed at my recollection of perching in front of the television in awe of newscasters as a teen. My reaction was to seize the pages from her hands—an act which startled her and even surprised me. Hearing her read aloud my youthful obsession with language while she was on the phone with another teenager made me feel vulnerable for reasons I can't quite explain. Yet the opportunity to read other authors' accounts of language and the opportunity to recall some of my own experiences was peculiarly liberating as I spent month after month in front of the computer. I would never have had the stories or the determination to complete this project in the wake of tremendous challenge if not for so many people some of whom I will name and others who know they are part of this undertaking. I am indebted to my parents Laverne and James who always told me to "talk louder"—and then gave me the "when the porch gets dry" story to tell for the rest of my life. To my sister Shirley and brother-in-law David, my aunt Alma S. Brown, Sharon R. Johnson, Elsie Byrd, Donna Stitt, Desiree Sterbini and Arlene Ferebee who encouraged my writing and/or gave me great stories to add to my own collection. To Karla Price who always called with a great "example" (especially the one from QVC "girl"). To Regina Fisher who makes me laugh with the "dranking" and stuff story. To Valerie Hayes and Eddison Bramble who showed me a whole new approach to the language of business during that amazing homecoming in Chapel Hill and the subsequent birthday celebration in New York. To Bobby McNeill who is always proud of me no matter what I have to say. To Anthony Jackson who says everything unflappably and to the great communicator, Teresa Blossom, who does not do enough sharing of her wonderful words with the public and therefore forces me to try to vicariously represent her talent through my own work. To Ditishia Simpson, my research assistant and to Dr. William Gay who said I should "do something" with my writing. To my best friend Nick Mackey (I know you can spell "restaurant") whose language is known to be "non-publishable" and who is probably at work now on his own book in order to keep the competition alive. To Marc Wallace who always stumbled across useful information for me and talked me through this project and to David Yorker the statistician extraordinaire who not only can always seem to "abra-ka-debra" me through my numerical challenges but seems to be listening to everything I say. To Joseph Major and Toria Burch who tolerated my frequent late-night telephone calls and allowed me to chatter from Times Square to Pawley's Island. And to Bryan Allen who, like me, never quite knew the art of spinning the story until now. To David Landrum, my "homey" (and my Miguel) who made me "bark" and encouraged me over and over again. To Amy Beddingfield who always remembered to bring the "letters." To Channelle James for giving me just the "right" tea talk to fuel this project and to Harry Mack, Tina Gordon and Tiffany Mitchell for the much-needed "therapy" and infinite anecdotes (I was "gone" call you!). To Tonya Carson, Freda McClain and Mamie Wilkins who know many of my stories. To the members and family I have at Trinity A.M.E.Z. Church who surround me with the faith I need to tell my story. And, finally to Brittany who by her own freedom as a teen who can spend a day chatting endlessly about nothing, unleashed my own autonomy and made it possible for me to have words on the following pages.

Introduction

Language sets people apart. Watch any primetime television show and that fact is starkly clear. Characters with southern accents, "foreign" accents and those who use formal English play distinguishably different roles. And, we think distinguishably different things about them. Who can forget the Clampett family whose mountaineer roots were reflected in their "hillbilly" references to "vittles"[1] or the James Bond[2] series, where Bond's discernible British accent sets him apart as slick opposition? The "valley girl" language popularized by at least one film, Clueless[3], enjoyed a long run in a host of popular television shows where popular girls were held in high social esteem. Visual electronic medium works to make the voices of people "familiar," often by utilizing codes imbedded in each production. Those codes, which I will discuss later in this work, reinforce Bourdieu's declaration (*On Television* 1996) that television is a medium that "enjoys a de facto monopoly on what goes into the heads of a significant part of the population and what they think" (18). One of the perils of those codes is the mistaking of them as truly characteristic of a population. Countless studies have demonstrated the veracity of this statement. Ella Shohat (1994) says that the "linguistics of domination" take into account that "English, especially, has often served as the linguistic vehicle for the projection of Anglo-American power, technology and finance." Calling language a "social battleground," Shohat adds that "language forms the site where political struggles are engaged both collectively and intimately."

---

1. The Beverly Hillbillies television show aired from 1962–1971. "Vittles" was their word for "food"
2. James Bond movies have existed from the 1950s to this current decade
3. Clueless is a 1995 film

My own experience has been that people mistake me for being white when they speak with me on the telephone. I have found this baffling over the years because I simply did not know what "white" sounds like. Yet, "sounding white" was having an impact on my navigation of space. For instance, one year during graduate school, I called the public library system to have a book held. When I arrived to pick up the book, I was informed by the elderly white library attendant that the book I requested was, in fact being held for one "Debra Smith." I responded that I, in fact, was Debra Smith to which the library representative responded, "honey, you sounded like a white girl on the phone." Beverly Tatum (1997) recalls a similar experience: "Following a presentation I gave to some educators, a white man approached me and told me how much he liked my ideas and how articulate I was. "You know," he concluded, "if I had had my eyes closed, I wouldn't have known it was a Black woman speaking" (Tatum 24). Meanwhile in the article "Sounding Black: Court-Sanctioned Racial Stereotyping" by Lis Wiehl, the author asks if you think you can determine someone's skin color by listening to his/her voice. Further, Wiehl asks "If so, would you swear to it in court? ... Would you testify to a defendant's guilt in a criminal trial based on listening to his voice and deciding on his race—never having seen him?" The article goes on to detail a Kentucky State Supreme Court ruling that "a white police officer, who had not seen the black defendant allegedly involved in a drug transaction, could, nevertheless, identify him as a participant by saying that a voice on an audiotape 'sounded black'.[4]

In another example of these same phenomena, I recall the experiences of my friend Arlene. During a volunteer project which involved transporting young black children to an activity, Arlene, a black woman, talked to the children in her vehicle about the activity in which they were about to partake. Along the way, she told them that they could tune the radio to any station they preferred. At one point while she was speaking, one of the children asked her "are you white?" Perplexed, because the child could clearly see her and therefore must be basing his inquiry upon her voice, Arlene asked him what he thought.

---

4. Wiehl, Lis. Harvard Blackletter Law Journal

He responded that she "looked" black. I believe that Arlene's proper English contributed to the child's inquiry, which could suggest that either he had no prior experience with black people speaking proper English, or he was socialized in some way to believe that proper English is only spoken by white people. Beverly Tatum (1997), writes about black children, who describe black scholarly, achievement-driven classmates as, "acting white." The author considers that their socialization has lent itself to their believing that the only studious, achieving people are, in fact, white. Therefore, for a black classmate to follow suit must indicate that they are mimicking white people. This concept is played out in a couple of examples on television. The "silenced" character is the term I use to describe that character who plays second-fiddle to the "star" of a situational comedy. "Carlton" from the *Fresh Prince of Bel Air*[5] and "Michael" from *Good Times*[6] are two examples. The former is hopeful about attending Princeton University even as he is an achiever in his senior year at the fictional Bel-Air High School. He speaks properly and is often chastised by his "cousin" Will (Will Smith, the star of the show) for being a "nerd." He is often seen in the company of white friends in contrast to Will's more masculine friends from "the hood." And, he goofily dances about to the music of Tom Jones. Donald Bogle (1992) says "Hollywood has never understood that there are many people from the inner city who can speak without slang (or who use it judiciously), who have manners and are perceptive enough to know when to talk loud and bad and when to sit back, listen and take in the scene before making any moves" (292–3). Prior to Carlton's marginalization, Michael from *Good Times* was often downplayed in favor of his brother J.J. (Jimmie Walker, the star of the show). While Michael spoke about Black Nationalism, and other political platforms, his exposure on screen played straight man (almost nerd) to his older brother's colorful antics. This reinforces the notion that intelligent roles are "nerdy" or "white." These characters are marginalized or play second fiddle or straight man to the more colorful characters' role.

---

5. Carlton Banks is the character portrayed by Alphonso Ribeira in the Fresh Prince of Bel Air which aired on television from 1990–1996.
6. Michael Evans is the character portrayed by Ralph Carter in Good Times which aired on television from 1974–1979.

While the "King's English" has typically been the language of power, popular culture has given way to new forms of power within language. In modern times, designers, liquor labels, department stores, and jewelers are prospering from the exposure they receive within the lyrics of rap music. This book examines the language of dominance, the language of hip-hop culture and the transition in power between the two genres. For more than twenty years now, rap artists have created a rivalry of sorts between those language staples of power and the opportunity for new forms of power in language, thus creating a space for us to examine new possibilities for linguistic capital.

I begin in **Chapter One**, *Language in Story*, by presenting a short story very loosely based upon my own experience with language. I conclude the chapter by providing an analysis of the five characters from the short story who confirm, challenge and deviate from the use of formal language. These characters, Virginia Carraway, Cathy Carraway, Becca Carraway, Belle Williams and Gerald Williams each offers some component of language that can be explored in depth and that are contributory to our beliefs about black people and language. **Chapter Two**, *Language in Television*, examines electronic media's role in language potential. The chapter examines the language of television that marks race especially for non-discriminating viewers like the young boy who interacted with my friend Arlene. In this chapter, I look at the function of characters like "Will Smith" and "Carlton Banks" in *The Fresh Prince of Bel Air* (1990s) and "Michael Evans" and "J.J. Evans" in *Good Times* (1970s). These four characters especially impart details about language based upon the characters they portray. **Chapter Three**, *Language in Hip-hop*, examines contemporary hip-hop language, often not standard English, and its marketability, while **Chapter Four**, *Language in Society* reveals the results of a survey taken to determine how the language of hip-hop and the language of business intersect, if at all. I conclude with **Chapter Five**, *Language Possibilities in the Classroom*, which discusses the possibilities inherent in language and how they can be played out in curriculum. Language certainly has possibility for pedagogy. The classroom instructor has a forum in which to change perceptions of language. Angela McRobbie says that "if representation remains a site of power and regulation, as well as a source of identity, then cultural academics working in the fields of representation have a critical job to do in attempting to recast these terms by inflecting new meanings" (McRobbie 726). Gray (1995) claims that culture can operate as a site of cultural politics as well as a source of cultural politics. Thus, he portends that there very well may be a relationship between representations and "the relationship of these representations to other discursive (and non-discursive) sites and practices" which include legal, theoretical and material (5). In this chapter I share some of the language stories from students and offer suggestions for curricular language inclusion.

In *Language and Symbolic Power*, Pierre Bourdieu considers that "the properties which characterize linguistic excellence may be summed up in two words: distinction and correctness." Yet, the words of authors Rickford and Rickford particularly motivated my research for this manuscript with regard to Black Vernacular English when they articulated:

> If we lost all of (the creative expression, culture and valued contained in Spoken Soul) in the heady pursuit of Standard English and the world of opportunities it offers, we would have indeed lost our soul. We are not convinced that African-Americans want to abandon "down home" speech in order to become one-dimensional speakers … Bear in mind that language is an inescapable element in almost everyone's daily life, and an integral element of human identity. If for that and no other reason, we would all do well to heed the still-evolving truth of the black language experience. That truth helps us confront one of the most critical questions of our day: Can one succeed in the wider world of economic and social power without surrendering one's distinctive identity?"[7]

After journeying through the variations in language, this work seeks to deliver powerful possibilities for language that are often unspoken.

---

7. Rickford and Rickford. Spoken Soul. Page 10.

The Words Unspoken

Chapter One

Language in Story

In the English language, black has typically been used to denote negativity: black market, black sheep, blackmail, etc. Shohat (1994) says that the "linguistics of domination" take into account that "English, especially, has often served as the linguistic vehicle for the projection of Anglo-American power, technology, and finance" (191). Shohat elaborates by saying "As a social battleground, language forms the site where political struggles are engaged both collectively and intimately. People do not enter simply into language as a master code; they participate in it as socially constituted subjects whose linguistic exchange is shaped by power relations (193). Following is a short story whose characters are intentionally linguistically distinguishable. In Chapter Two the primary story characters will be deconstructed to demonstrate the dynamism and determination of language.

* * *

Cathy heard the muffled sound of the telephone as she left the elevator. She hurriedly unlocked her apartment door. She hated to get telephone calls as soon as she arrived home. She dropped her briefcase and the brown paper bag that held tonight's dinner. The takeout container of shrimp-fried rice freed itself from the bag and plopped to the floor unopened, plastic fork landing beside it.

"Hello," she answered, glancing at her watch. Who could be calling at this hour? All of her friends were at aerobics class. She'd skipped it. She needed to be there, stepping, kicking and flinging her legs and arms to rid herself of the calories and guilt of a cheeseburger and beer spree enjoyed over the weekend. But she had reasons not to go. Besides the workload she needed to clear, it was raining. Rain was always a good excuse to stay at home and tend to long-delayed obligations and chores.

"Ms. Carraway?" a high-pitched voice asked.

"Speaking," she replied, raising one dark eyebrow. The voice was unfamiliar, and she feared a solicitation to change her long-distance telephone carrier.

"This is Chris Thomas from McLeod College. Dr. Donovan Burke's secretary."

"Oh, of course. How are you?"

"Fine, thanks. Ms. Carraway, I'm calling all of the candidates for the Distinguished Professor of English and Literature for next year. Dr. Burke and the search team have completed the preliminary screening, and you're among the candidates they now want to interview for the position."

Cathy listened intently to the woman on the other end. She dropped her black leather coach bag on the floor and sat down beside it. "All right," she said. "When?"

"Dr. Burke wants to set up a conference call with you, himself, and members of the search committee. With the difference in time zones, I'm calling to find out when before noon your time would be good for you, say on Wednesday and Thursday of this week?"

Cathy hesitated for a moment, twirling her curly light brown hair around her finger. Quickly, she made a mental review of her schedule for the week.

"Wednesday," she lied in a cheerful voice. She rolled her hazel green eyes at the thought of getting up really early in the morning. At least she wouldn't have to shower or dress for the interview.

"There's an eight or eight-thirty slot still open on Dr. Burke's calendar," Chris said. "Gee, that would be six or six-thirty your time, though. I wish there was something else, but I'm sorry. He's really booked—"

"I understand," Cathy assured her. "Look, put me on his calendar for eight a.m. on Wednesday. It's really not a problem as long as you call me at this number."

"All right," Chris agreed doubtfully. "The conference call operator will call you at this number on Wednesday morning at six a.m., your time for your interview with Dr. Burke and the others."

"Is there any additional material or anything else Dr. Burke needs from me before Wednesday?"

"No, and as soon as I confirm the other participants later today, I'll fax a list to you so you'll know who'll be part of the interview."

"Great. I'd appreciate that," Cathy said, and Chris said goodbye.

Cathy reached for her briefcase and pulled out her résumé with her right hand. At the same time, she grabbed the container of rice by the wire handle with her left.

"Catherine Leanna Carraway," she read from the top of the résumé. She eyed her credentials on the page. She paused at the degrees that made Robert and Virginia Carraway so proud.

She could hear her mother bragging to friends about "the doctor of education in the family." Her father's pride was quieter in both Cathy and her brother. He'd silently paid the bills not covered by their scholarships to the University of Wisconsin, just around the corner from their home. She had lived with her parents while earning all three degrees. She had never needed to ask for money. Robert Carraway had simply provided it, along with the small foreign sedan and deposit on the apartment when she decided to leave home. Even more important to Cathy, he had sometimes consulted her on business matters, which showed his confidence in her abilities. Although his words to her were few, Cathy always felt his pride and support.

Virginia's boasting embarrassed Cathy. She always introduced her daughter as "Dr. Carraway." She also insisted that the secretary at St. Paul's Baptist, whose congregation included a large section of the city's most moneyed professionals, list Cathy as "doctor" Carraway on the church program. Cathy felt uncomfortable using the title generally associated with medical practitioners. Occasionally, people would enter into conversation with her just to ask about a sore throat, stiff shoulder, or other ailment. They seemed to walk away either in disappointment or discomfort after Cathy's apologies at not being able to help. Still, Virginia did not understand her daughter's protests.

"After all," Virginia would rationalize, "you've earned that doctorate, honey, and I want everyone in Madison to know it."

Cathy sighed. She did have good parents. But at 28 it was time to get out of Madison and see what the rest of the world looked like. McLeod College, located in a small city in Georgia, might be her first destination.

Cathy finished eating and tidied the living room area of her one-bedroom apartment. She headed for the bathroom to wash her face and change clothes, loosening the buttons on her blouse and skirt as she walked. Finishing up in the bathroom, she bypassed the television in her bedroom and opted for the book lying on the bedside table. Cathy eyed the cover and flipped back to the page where she'd stopped the night before. She knew the work in her briefcase was calling, but she couldn't resist her favorite author....

* * *

Belle Williams read the memo that lay in her in-box upon her arrival at her office after her morning classes. "Four candidates have been selected based upon their educational credentials, experience, and professional standing. Chris has set up a schedule for us to interview each candidate. Because two of the candidates are not local, their interviews will be conducted by conference call ..."

Belle skimmed the memo and stopped at the names: Pamela Avery, Catherine Leanna Carraway, Pat Schilhavy, and Grace Wavell. Shaking her head, she set the memo down on the corner of her desk.

Belle Williams was an attractive woman despite her constant scowl of disbelief. "I believe half of what I hear and all of what I see," was her motto at McLeod College. Although she was tough on her students, every so often one of them could coax a smile to her full lips which were always bare except for a dab of Vaseline.

It was an odd thing, helping to replace oneself. Belle had hoped that her father would adjust to the senior care home where she'd moved him two years ago. But, he hated the place, and his doctors agreed that his temperament was hampering his recovery from the stroke. Belle had decided to bring her father back home, which was what he wanted, and to care for him herself with the help of a part-time nurse. In familiar, beloved surroundings, Belle knew her father would recover within a year or two.

Her plan required cutting back on her teaching load until then, and though the Chair of the English department hesitated at first, Belle was too valuable for the college to lose. Two of her books had become national bestsellers, and she was a prolific publisher. She sat on the board of a governor's commission on education and had been invited to the White House by two different presidents for her expertise. So, when Belle Williams said she would have to limit her teaching schedule which would require that someone else be hired to take on the balance of her classes, the Chair of the English Department agreed, and Belle made arrangements to bring her father home.

She was disappointed that more candidates had not applied for the job. McLeod College was small, but its reputation was as strong as the backs of the newly freed slaves that had built the school in 1866. Belle felt a part of the tradition built by those determined men and women. She had hoped more potential candidates would have felt the same.

So far, she had been displeased. Only a few applicants were from the South at all, much less Georgia. Belle understood that young people preferred Wall Street and Washington careers or entrepreneurial pursuits over teaching these days. Everyone wanted to be the next Bill Gates, Donald Trump, or Mrs. Fields. She could hardly blame them. If not for her book royalties and speaking fees, she could not afford the medical bills that her father's Medicare did not cover.

It had not been difficult to narrow the field to four candidates. She knew two of them personally. Both Grace Wavell and Pamela Avery were well-known outside education. Belle had reasons to oppose them both. Grace was a capable lecturer in freshman English and Journalism at a North Carolina college. But, the woman had never published anything of academic significance. Worse, her master's degree was in Anthropology—a result of a decision to remain in school and pursue the man of her dreams at that time, who just happened to be the Chair of the Anthropology Department. Unfortunately, as far as Belle was concerned, Grace's name was practically a household word in the Bible Belt because of her opposition to rap music. As a former reporter herself, Grace knew how to attract and hold media attention. She staged rallies at major record stores and urged boycotts of rap music labels. She had sound bites down pat. Her work might have value as cultural commentary—although Belle had her doubts about that—but it lacked scholarly staying power. Belle had no doubt that Grace Wavell would soon be as well known as the critics of disco.

Pamela Avery wrote intellectual tomes published by the Edison Foundation and other educational forums. Her research credentials were impeccable. Indeed, she had collaborated on one project with

Belle, a study of the impact of desegregation on education in rural Georgia schools. The problem was that, despite her dual doctorate in education and economics, Pamela had not taught for nearly twelve years. Her expertise lay in administration. She had long ago left the classroom for the chancellor's office and later won a precinct seat on the school board. Belle saw clearly the political advantages that drew Pamela to the vacancy at McLeod. The college could brag about attracting the superintendent of the state's most respected school district. And Pamela could use McLeod's community support among grassroots voters to propel herself into either a congressional seat or the Atlanta mayoral office during the next election.

As much as she dreaded having Grace or Pamela at McLeod, Belle knew she might have to support one of them. At least she knew them. No one at McLeod had ever heard of Catherine Leanna Carraway or Pat Schilhavy before receiving their vitae. The search committee had picked them because they met the degree requirements, would not cost the college much in salary, and they were unknown. Unlike Pamela, Grace, and Belle herself, Catherine Carraway and Pat Schilhavy presented no danger of outshining the rest of the McLeod faculty.

Belle was no fool. She knew some colleagues resented her achievements and the national attention they afforded her. She attracted more endowments to the college than any other staff member. The criticisms—from the women that she was too pushy—from the men that her expectations were too high—from the whites that she spent too much of the school's money on airfare—had hurt at first. Over the years, she became immune to the criticisms, and even the most jealous among her colleagues never challenged Belle Williams' loyalty to the college or her students. And, after all, she had sacrificed her marriage for them.

She realized now that her loyalty might force her to make a deal with whichever woman she decided represented the lesser of two evils. She mentally gagged at the prospect. The bottom line was they were both white women. Belle hated these games.

She took a few minutes to read all the vitae again. Who would help McLeod College and the students the most? Someone who was much like them was the answer that always came to Belle's mind. The résumés had offered her no clear choice. Putting the papers aside, Belle picked up the phone.

"Hi Chris. No, I don't need to speak to him. As a matter of fact, I was hoping to talk to you if you have a minute."

* * *

The steam from the showers made it difficult for Cathy to keep her hair from curling. She resumed her street clothes. She felt revived from her workout at the gym.

"Have ya tol' your parents yet?" asked her sister-in-law Becca, who was already dressed. She admired the way each honey-brown curl fell over Cathy's forehead. Becca's voice was hesitant, which was usual for the woman Robert had married seven years ago. He had been stationed at Pope Air Force base when he met her. They married soon afterwards, and Cathy felt no surprise when their child was born well before their nine-month anniversary. Rebecca was a sweet but weak girl who had married straight out of high school. Growing up near the military base, she had always seen a soldier husband, not education, as her only opportunity to escape the trailer park and find a secure future. She was not the wife Robert needed, and Virginia rarely missed an opportunity to remind her of the fact. Her mother-in-law's disapproval increased Becca's nervous efforts at ingratiation. She filled in whenever Robert Sr. needed help at the office, ran errands for Virginia, and exercised three times a week with Cathy. Only two years separated them in age, a gap that Becca's experience as a wife and mother should have filled. It hadn't. They had few mutual interests, and their conversation usually died within five minutes. As much as she tried to like Becca, Cathy silently agreed with her mother that perhaps Becca should seek higher education. She did not consider Becca a friend, yet the younger woman had still joined Cathy's exercise spa.

Cathy slid her slender feet into a pair of black leather shoes with suede accents. "I thought after dinner tonight," she answered. Becca's expression turned to horror.

"But, I'll be there," she protested around a piece of gum.

Cathy knew that Becca did not want to be near her mother-in-law when she broke the news.

"We'll be in the living room. You can offer to clear the table and hide in the kitchen," Cathy said dryly.

"Yeah, good," she smiled. "Then I can help Josh with his bath and stay in his room."

Cathy put the combination lock in her exercise bag and closed the locker. She almost laughed at Becca's pathetic, relieved expression. Her own longing to escape her mother's disapproval stopped her.

* * *

The orderly wheeled the dinner cart down the hall. Belle sat by her father's bed, spooning the spaghetti into his mouth. He beamed with enjoyment.

"I cleaned out yo' ole room, papa," she told him softly as she fed him. She often came by at dinner. Her company calmed him, and he would sleep better during the night. "Ya know dat ole quilt of Mama Nell's? I hung it on da back wall so you can see it first thing you get up and last thing at night." He smiled and nodded, shaking lose a small bit of pasta. Belle used her finger to gently urge it back to his lips. "Papa, now dat you coming home, I thought you might could help me with my next book. I've been thinking mo' and mo' bout all those stories you used to tell me about McLeod in the early days. Me and you could go talk about what you remember from dem days and some of what my momma used to tell. Maybe Mr. and Mrs. Onessa Scott, they wouldn't mind talking either. I could maybe tape it and den put it all down on paper."

Her voice, smooth as Georgia moonshine, continued soothing her father, long after the orderly returned to remove the empty dinner tray and settle Mr. Williams for the night.

* * *

The sound of dishes crashing drifted into the living room where the Carraways sat over coffee. Cathy cringed. Becca's nervousness had been apparent throughout the meal, and her furtive glances at Cathy had not gone unnoticed.

"My goodness gracious," Virginia Carraway muttered, making to rise. "I sure hope she hasn't broken another china place setting—"

"It's okay." Becca called out from the kitchen. A clattering cascade of silverware against ceramic tile and then a giggle from Joshua followed. "Everything's okay! Don't ya'll disturb yourselves."

Virginia stood with determination. "I'd better go see for myself."

Her husband waved her back onto the sofa. "Let the girl be, Ginny. Besides, don't you want to hear what Cathy's got to say?"

Robert Carraway amazed his daughter. He always knew when she was holding something back. Countless times he had told her to "Spit it out" when she was a young girl struggling for the right words or trying to frame her disagreement or anger respectfully.

"What do you mean, Cathy wants to say something? We just finished having a perfectly good conversation during dinner. I thought we came in here to watch 'Wheel of Fortune.' Do you want sugar in your coffee tonight, Robert?"

"I could do with a spoonful."

"What about you, Cathy dear?" Virginia handed the cup to her husband. "Is something happening at the university? Don't tell me they're going to make you a full professor after all?"

"No, mother. And no coffee for me, thanks. I'm trying to give it up."

"Humph," her mother said, sitting back with her own creamed coffee. "Then what is it? Or was your father joking?"

"There's some good news that I wanted to share—"

Virginia put her cup down in excitement, clasping her pale hands together. "You're getting married!"

"No! I mean, mother, where in the world did that come from? I'm not even seeing anyone right now."

"What about that nice man from church? Adam or Alan—I never get it right."

"His name was Andrew, mother. We stopped dating months ago."

"Such a nice young man," her mother added, taking another sip of coffee. "Attractive, and a dentist, too. I'll bet he makes at least six figures a year in his practice."

Cathy exchanged an impatient look with her father, who shrugged and hid a smile behind his coffee cup.

"Well, I've decided to leave U-W. Right now, I'm an associate professor there, and I've been looking for an opportunity to grow professionally." she explained.

"Sounds good," her father said.

"That's wonderful" said Virginia. "Just the other day, I was saying to Becca that she should go back to school and improve herself. Marquette has that wonderful adult learning school. Wouldn't it be great if the two of you were at Marquette together?"

Cathy could think of better things, like lying in the middle of the I-94 freeway. "Actually, I thought I'd get away from Wisconsin schools. In fact, I've got an interview in the morning, and, if it goes well, I'll be visiting a Georgia college later this month."

"Well, congratulations, honey," her father said.

Virginia set her coffee down with a snap. "Excuse me?"

"You heard the girl, Ginny," her husband said. "This is great news, Cathy. Great news."

"You have an interview in the morning?" her mother asked sharply.

"Yes. The search committee is going to interview me by conference call—"

"But, Georgia?" Virginia pounced again. "Why on earth would you want to move there?"

"They're offering a distinguished professorship," Cathy explained.

"But they haven't offered it to you yet, is that right?"

"No, but I'm one of four candidates, so I'm optimistic. It's a wonderful opportunity."

"Of course," her mother conceded, "it's just that you want to keep your options open. You know, there are other colleges in Wisconsin besides Marquette."

"Ginny," her husband said sternly.

"I'm only trying to say—"

"Oh, I think we know what you're saying," Robert said wryly. "So Cathy, tell us about the school. Georgia, right? The weather's enough of a recommendation. I'll bet we'll still have snow on the ground every Easter when you're out riding your bicycle down there."

"The school's called McLeod College. It's a traditionally black school—" Cathy hurried on.

"Black—?"

"Ginny."

"Listen, Robert—"

"Stop interrupting the girl, Ginny. It's a wonderful school. Didn't the last Secretary of Commerce graduate from there?"

"But—"

"I believe he did. And that actress who got nominated a couple years ago for an Oscar. You really picked a good school, Cathy."

"Thanks," Cathy said and quickly told her parents what she knew about the academic program at McLeod. She had no idea if any graduates of McLeod had ever become presidential appointees or Hollywood stars, but she appreciated her father for saying so.

* * *

Belle entered Dr. Burke's office ten minutes before the conference call was scheduled.

"Don," she began without preamble, "has anyone ever seen this woman?"

"Good morning to you, too, Belle," Donovan Burke mocked her gently over his thick, dark frames. "What woman are we talking about, exactly?"

"The one we're interviewing this morning. This Catherine Carraway."

"I haven't. Sue's heard of her. Has a colleague at U-W that had her in his class. Said she was an excellent student. Unfortunately, at least unfortunately for her, Wisconsin doesn't believe in building its distinguished faculty from the students who graduate from there. Think they need more diversity—people from other universities. That's why she's interested in this position."

"And," Belle said, picking up a pile of papers from a chair and sitting down.

"And, what?" Donovan asked, but the phone interrupted him.

It was the conference call operator. Donovan put the call on the speaker, and Belle's point went unheard as the operator added the other participants. Catherine Carraway joined the line last.

* * *

Cathy doodled on the paper in front of her. She could not identify the voices. They all sounded distant and hollow. She'd answered several questions about classroom technique and course content. The questions were easy and Cathy answered them easily. Then, the woman's voice returned to the attack.

"How do you feel 'bout teaching at a black college? Would you feel out of place at all?"

"What do you mean?"

"I mean," the tone turned more aggressive, "McLeod is predominately black—both da school and da community. You're in a place dats jus' the opposite. Da University of Wisconsin has what? Five percent, maybe eight percent minority student population? At McLeod—"

"About nine percent actually," Cathy corrected her.

"—we got a seventy-five percent black student body. Da faculty's mostly black too. We're not exactly what you're used to, are we?"

"No," Cathy admitted. "But none of what you've mentioned has any bearing on my ability to teach or the students' abilities to learn—"

"Really?"

"Yes, really. Excuse me, but is this Professor Burton or Williams?" They were the only two women on Cathy's list.

"Williams."

"Well, Professor Williams, as far as the diverse composition of the campus population goes, frankly, that's one of the attractions. You haven't mentioned budgets yet, but I assure you I do know that McLeod's financial resources don't compare to U-W's. Yet, McLeod's academics are top-notch. Whatever the challenges, both faculty and students seem to conquer them. I look forward to being part of a team like that."

"You've lived all your life in Wisconsin, Ms. Carraway?"

"Yes."

"Do you have any concerns about living in da' Souf?"

"Of course, I'd be interested in housing and recreational facilities. I'm familiar with Atlanta, but not many other cities in Georgia, including McLeod."

"Georgia is still mostly small towns, Ms. Carraway," the same female voice said. "Da Souf is da heart of the Bible Belt. People here tend to be conservative."

"I was raised by Southern Baptists myself," Cathy answered. "I don't think it did me any lasting damage."

A few people laughed.

* * *

Rolling green fields sparkled with annuals lovingly tended by the landscaping crew. A student parking his moped caused the bicycles to tumble. Construction workers framed the shell that would be the new undergraduate library.

Inside the English building, Cathy faced her first class of the day.

Though she tried to wash away her anger in the shower, some still lingered from Belle Williams' cross-examination. The woman's harsh words echoed in Cathy's head, and for the first time in weeks, she scrutinized each student sitting in front of her.

There were two black students, three Asians, and maybe one Latino in a lecture hall of seventy students. What, Cathy wondered, would Belle Williams make of this picture? What would she say?

Restless noises—papers rustling, books closing, throats clearing—brought Cathy's attention back to her students.

"This morning, we're going to take a look at the way we use language. I know you think we're always using language, but how do we use it? Often, the language we use fits our goals at the time. We have 'lines' for every situation, don't we? Hang out at the Quad," she named a popular college club, "and you'll hear all kinds of lines, especially around closing time when people don't want to go home alone." Some students laughed. "There is a language for romance, a language for business, a language we use in religion. And what about the words we use? Can anyone tell me how many words there are in the English language?"

"Too many," someone muttered.

"Be more specific," Cathy urged. "Come on, I know you're not math majors, but surely you remember what numbers are?"

"Eight thousand," someone called.

"Twenty thousand," another suggested.

"Higher," Cathy urged them.

"A million!"

"Lower," she called, moving to the blackboard.

"Half a million?"

"Okay, close enough. Actually, six hundred thousand." She wrote the number on the board and drew an arrow beside it. "And how many of these six hundred thousand words do we use?" She looked around the lecture hall. The students shouted different numbers. "Five hundred, according to research conducted by Bone and Robertson in 1994," she answered above the noise and added the number to the board among gasps and mutters of disbelief.

"No way!" a student called.

"Way!" Cathy disagreed, adding a second arrow and a new number. "And those words have fifteen hundred definitions. Definitions, that can differ depending on what region you live in or your age, your sex, your race."

Cathy circled the five hundred, then turned to face the class again, walking to the edge of the lecture platform. "We've got this ocean of words that comprise our language, but we're all swimming in this very small pool of five hundred words. So, what are we really talking about when we talk about language? How should we define it? Should we be talking about the spoken word or the unspoken?"

* * *

Belle spoke urgently into the phone. "Pam, unless you show that you're serious, she's the one they're leaning towards. They jus' ate her up with all her proper talk. Look, we're already at 55-45. If we hire another white professor we'll be dead even, for pete's sake. Let's give these kids a role model. I don't mind so much about her high-class talk, but a white Distinguished Professor of English and Literature is not exactly what I had in mind as my replacement."

"You know I empathize, Belle. You know I do—"

"You can't pull out."

"I'm not. It's just that our poll shows I need more support from voters between 25 and 35. And their children are in elementary schools, not college."

"One semester, Pam. We could convince Don to make the position a visiting distinguished professorship. That will at least give me a chance to get my father settled and put the word out."

"One semester? That's it?"

"Yes."

"Let me run it by my people, and get back with you."

* * *

A tingle ran up Robert Carraway's arm, causing him to grimace.

"You sure you alwright? I can run to the store and get you something. My car's right in front on the skreet."

"Becca, stop giving your space to Sophie Wallace. She can park on the street instead of in the lot."

"It's just temporary, Mr. Carraway. She twisted her ankle the other day—"

"That girl is always twisting something so she can talk you out of your parking space."

"I don't mind none. She nice enough about it. Besides, it's easier to just run out when it's time to bring everybody's lunch back."

The printer light flashed. "See? It comes out here in a few seconds."

"And I just hit these two buttons?"

"Right. Or use this here mouse and go under file to get the print command."

"Okay"

"Now, you sure you don't want nothing?"

"No, thank you very much Becca. I don't want anything. I'm probably just tired and my arm fell asleep before the rest of me."

* * *

Virginia Carraway was waiting for her daughter in the apartment lobby that night. Cathy sighed when she saw her. She had a brief urge to get back in the car and hope her mother hadn't seen her. But her mother had been watching for Cathy's arrival and was now looking right at her.

She waved, and Cathy forced a smile. She should have expected this. Virginia Carraway had made her disapproval apparent the other night. Obviously, she had been waiting to talk to Cathy away from her husband's interference.

"I do like that briefcase," Virginia said as they rode in the elevator. "So distinguished, but still very feminine. Did I give it to you for your birthday or Christmas?"

"Birthday."

"Of course. Two years ago, wasn't it? I must say it still looks new."

"Can I get you something to drink?" Cathy offered as they went into the apartment.

"No, you go change into something more comfortable, dear." She opened the refrigerator. "I'll put together a little something for both of us."

Cathy retreated to the bedroom. She needed a shower and a change of clothes before sitting down to a meal with her mother.

Returning to the kitchen, Cathy sniffed the air with appreciation. Years as a housekeeper had enabled Virginia to turn the scant contents of her refrigerator into a savory meal.

"Cathy, you really need to go to the grocery store." Virginia put the plates, with their slivers of beef with steamed broccoli and potatoes, onto the small table. She filled their glasses with iced herbal tea.

Now," she began after grace, "I talked to Mary Alice Tate today. You know her husband's a tenured professor at Marquette, and I told her about your situation. Now she said ..."

Cathy listened without hearing Virginia's words. Sometimes, she forgot that her mother had grown up in the cotton fields of North Carolina. In 1970s Wisconsin, Cathy had grown up speaking the language of her parents, a mix of English tinged with Southern dialect. Her parents had both graduated from a small Carolina college, but could not get a white-collar job in their native South. Her mother became a maid at the local Women's Club and her father took up the ministry. They saved enough to move to Wisconsin before Cathy was born. Her parents started a maintenance company that flourished. Cathy and her brother, Robert Jr., the elder by five years, began to get the best that money could buy, including a television set. But while the rest of America tuned into the box for entertainment, Cathy's parents forced their children to watch the evening news and repeat the words of John Chancellor, David Brinkley, and Walter Cronkite. They watched nothing else. It was how her entire family learned to talk "right." Robert Sr. erased his drawl and talked his way into cleaning contracts with local office towers and automotive dealerships. Virginia never quite lost her accent, which, Cathy guessed, only strengthened her determination for her children. Instead, she assumed the air of the rich women whose houses she had once cleaned. Her mother, however, was not a clever mimic. She sounded like Jackie Onassis one moment, Dinah Shore the next. Her affectation confused, alienated or, to Virginia's dismay, amused many listeners.

Cathy wondered if Virginia's influence had been what led her to study English and to take education courses. If so, Virginia could not help but be disappointed at Cathy's tolerance for the changing reality of language. To Cathy, language was a living, growing thing. It was not the stagnant form that Virginia demanded. Her mother wanted the words to be the same on everyone's tongue. If they weren't, then the person was not worth listening to. Becca was proof of this belief.

But Cathy knew that kids hanging on street corners could take a language, hold it in their hands, and reshape it. How else could a billion-dollar industry like rap emerge from South Central Los Angeles?

Cathy gained an unexpected benefit from having newscasters as her tutors. She absorbed a wealth of knowledge about national and world politics, history, and culture with each newscaster's cadence and elocution. Both she and Robert had graduated at the top of their high school classes and in the top one-percent at the University of Wisconsin. Rob Jr. joined the Air Force, fulfilling a dream inspired by the "Star Wars" trilogy. If he could not become a Jedi knight, then a fighter pilot was the next best thing.

She rarely watched television these days. Her hectic schedule left little room for diversion. When she needed relaxation, she preferred listening to the radio or playing an old album. Andrew never understood her apathy toward TV. Cathy had not always been disinterested. She had worked to achieve that cool state. At one point, she refused even to own a television, she hated it so. But maturity had shown her that television had been her mother's messenger. Her hatred for the medium was misplaced.

"Cathy, are you listening to me?"

"Yes, mother" she answered. "I've heard every word."

* * *

Virginia left after cleaning up the kitchen, and Cathy settled down to grading papers, trying to distract herself from her mother's visit. On one paper, she suggested that the student consult two chapters on regional dialects in Labelle Macheau's book, *An Uncommon Tongue:*

Regional Interpretations of English in the United States. The reclusive author was one of her favorites.

The phone rang before she finished the stack.

"God," she groaned, fearing her mother's voice. "Hello?"

"Ms. Carraway? Professor Carraway?"

"Yes?"

"This is Mark Simmons from McLeod. With the search committee. We spoke earlier."

"Oh. Yes, of course. Good evening Professor Simmons."

"Call me Mark, please, Catherine. I— I suppose you're wondering why I'm calling?"

"Was there some more information you needed?"

"No. I just wanted to you to know that I thought you did very well in the interview this morning."

"Thank you. It was an interesting interview—"

"You didn't let Belle Williams throw you. She intimidates a lot of people. I can tell you, the committee is very impressed that you stood up to her."

"I don't know about that. I did try to answer her questions honestly."

"You did very well. In fact, I think you'd be a great addition to our staff."

"Well thank you. I appreciate that."

"You'd like McLeod. It's a lot warmer here than in Wisconsin."

"Yes, I know."

"Well, I just wanted to give you my vote of confidence."

* * *

The student across from Belle felt terrified, and it showed.

"You're not working up to yo' potential, Samantha. This," she tossed a recent assignment across the desk, "is 'D' work."

"I'm sorry, Professor Williams."

"Why apologize to me? I got my college degree. In fact, I got several. You're the one who hasn't got a degree, and you'll not likely get one with this kind of shoddy work."

"I'm sorr— I mean, I'll do better."

"You said that last time. I believe half of what I hear and all of what I see."

"I mean it. I really do."

"There are a lot of kids dying to come to McLeod. A lot of them want to sit right where you're sitting."

"I know."

"You want to tell me what's wrong?"

"Huh? I mean, what?"

"The reason yo' grades are slipping this semester. I checked with your advisor befo' calling you in here. Your grades have dropped in everything 'cept your Phys Ed class."

"It's just temporary."

Belle didn't answer. She simply eyed the young woman in the silence.

"I'll work harder," the student promised.

"Look," Belle began bluntly. "If it's drugs, clean yourself up. If it's a man, get rid of him. Nothing is worth risking your education. Do you understand?"

"Yes ma'am."

"You'd better."

* * *

Cathy appreciated Mark's encouragement and information about the college. He had really appeared to genuinely like her in the short telephone conversation. And, it was nice to have an ally at McLeod. But why did he deliberately seem to be pitting her against Belle Williams? And, wasn't it unethical for a member of the search committee to call to offer his vote of support? She tried to clear her thoughts of Mark Simmons as she pulled back the covers and climbed into bed.

* * *

The search committee had been discussing their evaluations of the candidates for more than an hour without reaching a decision.

"Let's invite them all to campus," someone suggested.

"We can't afford to invite all four. We need to narrow it to the one or two we think are suited to the job and likely to take it."

"The Carraway woman knows her stuff," another member said. "She seems ambitious, interested in making a name for herself."

"Does that mean she'll move here and start looking for her next job?" Belle asked, and there were murmurs of agreement in the room.

"That's always a risk," Donovan pointed out. "But I think the Distinguished Professorship is incentive enough to keep her here for awhile. After all, she is anxious to leave a fine institution to come to McLeod."

"Pamela has already published distinguished research papers," Belle said.

"We need teachers, not researchers," someone grumbled.

"We need both," Belle insisted. "Research helps keep our accreditation. Besides, McLeod students need role models and the role models need to look like them."

"We need someone we can afford," another emphasized. "Carraway's asking a salary we can pay. Some of the others have us confused with Georgia Tech."

"Both Dr. Avery and Ms. Wavell are willing to forgo some salary for other considerations."

"Yeah, like time off to pursue other interests," Mark Simmons said. "Excuse me, Belle, but we need someone who's going to be here day in and day out. Like you, I would prefer a stallion, but right now, we need a workhorse."

* * *

Cathy took the slice of pepperoni pizza out of the microwave and added it to her plate of salad. The phone rang as she took the first bite.

"That you, Cat?"

"Rob!" she screamed with delight. "Where are you?"

"No place you want to know about," her brother answered. A member of a tactical strike team, he often went into political hot spots that he could not talk about with his family. "Look, I don't have much time. Becca tells me you're moving to Georgia?"

She laughed at his enthusiasm. "Maybe. I'll know in a few days. I'm pretty excited.

"So," he said. "Talk to me. Tell me what else's been going on. If you're moving, I guess you're not about to get married or anything?"

She laughed and shared what news she knew. "You should come home more often," Cathy chided her brother.

"Now you sound like Becca," he sighed. "God, I miss her. And Josh, too."

"And they miss you. We all do."

* * *

That night, Cathy dreamed she was climbing. She went higher and higher into the elm tree in the backyard. She knew it was forbidden, yet she kept going.

"Catherine Leanna Carraway!" The scream came from the back door, and she heard running feet—big ones and small ones.

"Cathy?" That was Rob's voice, gentle and coaxing. "Can you make it down?"

She looked back over her route. "No."

"Oh dear Jesus." Her mother, a Southern Baptist, crossed herself, imitating a Catholic woman she had once worked for.

Cathy looked down to tell them, don't worry. Then her foot slipped off the branch.

"Robert!" Her wide eyes watched her daughter's thin arms cling to the branch. "Robert, we need you!"

"What is it?" his father called.

"Cathy's about to fall. Hurry!"

The screen door slammed. Rob glanced over his shoulder. His father would never cross the distance in time.

"Cathy," he said gently, his eyes holding hers. He lifted his arms. "Come on."

And she let go, to the sound of her mother's screams and her father's thudding run. She wasn't afraid. She never doubted Rob would catch her.

Her weight sent them both crashing to the ground. But there were no broken bones and no tears.

She was six to his eleven, and her brother had been her hero ever since.

* * *

Belle sat with her father on the porch swing. She tucked the blanket around his knees.

"Ursuwayson," he said.

"Yes, papa," Belle sniffed the air. "It's gonna rain real soon. Probably by morning."

* * *

A soft rain tickled the pane. For three days, the Northern Midwest had been treated to an unrelenting rainfall.

The bright colors of Joshua's room contrasted to the gray Saturday afternoon. His aunt drew happy giggles from him as they took turns reading the new book she'd brought him.

Cathy spent many hours reading in this room. It had been hers before she'd decided to move.

"'Brer Rabbit ain't goin' ter do nothin' no more!'" Cathy growled.

"'Did is de end! Brer Rabbit is dead!'" Josh read.

"'But right den, Brer Fox an Brer Bear hear a scufflin' mongst de leaves, way at—'"

"What is going on here?" Virginia demanded from the doorway.

"Grandmother, Aunt Cathy got me a new book. See my new book?" He held up a copy of Walt Disney's Uncle Remus Stories. "And it's not my birthday or anything."

Virginia's narrow glance went from the book to her daughter. "That's what you brought him?"

"Yes. We were just reading this funny story about a rabbit."

"Not anymore." Virginia snatched the book from her grandson's hands.

"Mine!" Josh cried.

"Mother!" Cathy protested in disbelief.

"Josh, you are not to cry like a baby. Go into the bathroom and wash your face."

The little boy sniffled. His bottom lip trembling, he crawled off the bed. "Yes, ma'am," he stammered and left the room.

As soon as the bathroom door closed, Cathy turned angrily to her mother. "What the hell is wrong with you? Why'd you take his book like that?"

"Catherine, you are talking to your mother, so I'll thank you not to curse."

"Give me the book, mother," Cathy commanded through clenched teeth.

"I will not. You never should have given it to him in the first place. You know he's still developing his motor and speech skills. I will not have him talking like some 'Uncle Remus' character."

"It's a classic book. Lots of kids read it."

"Not my grandson," Virginia Carraway declared.

Cathy closed her eyes in dismay. She could see Virginia working on the boy, trying to mold her grandson as she had done his father and aunt. Rob's wife was no match for Virginia. Becca was one of the few cowed by Virginia's tone. Her own aspirations as a child had been lowered by poor self-esteem. Virginia was well aware of that fact. And Becca's lack of education only made the ground more fertile for Virginia's brand of intimidation.

"Give me the book, mother."

"Let's see what Becca has to say about this."

"You can't stop me from reading to him at my place."

"Then it's a good thing you may be moving soon, isn't it?"

* * *

Thunderous applause sounded as Belle Williams answered the last question. Her speech had earned a standing ovation before she took questions from a dozen audience members, who were now lining up for her to sign copies of her books.

As the line thinned, Belle noticed Grace Wavell watching the scene.

"You're a legend to your fans, Belle," Grace greeted her. "Even after all these years."

"Hello, Grace. Are you covering the conference or just throwing bricks at the intellectuals?"

"Can I help it if Ph.D.'s sound so pompous? Not you, of course. You've got that downhome charm."

"Next you'll be complimenting my work." Belle managed a tight smile as she collected her purse.

"Your speech wasn't too bad," Grace acknowledged. "By the way, I ran into Mark Simmons down the hall. He told me the committee is close to a decision."

"We are."

"He went on and on about the need for new blood, the need for more diversity. I got the distinct feeling he wanted someone a lot lighter than me."

"Mark's entitled to his own opinion," Belle increased her stride. "But he doesn't speak for the College."

"I would hope not. If Mark had his way, there'd be so much diversity, there'd be no black colleges left."

"Like I said, Mark is entitled to his own opinions. It's a free world."

* * *

Robert Carraway left after breakfast so that Virginia could inspect the house. The Rev. Adam Brooks, the guest of honor, expected first-class treatment from his flock.

Becca trailed Virginia Carraway from room to room as the elder woman inspected the house in preparation for the minister at St. Paul's coming for Sunday dinner.

"We thought we do the new uniforms—"

"We would do, dear," Mrs. Carraway corrected.

"Oh, yes m'am. We would do," she repeated obediently, "them in a different color. More distinct."

"Distinctive. And do be careful of what you say around Joshua, Rebecca. Why, today he actually called me "grammaw" or something. Just what are you saying to him? You know I prefer grandmother."

"Yes, m'am," Becca agreed, absently looking around the room.

"Would you look at this dust?" Mrs. Carraway asked, revealing the speck from an encyclopedia volume in the bookcase. "I need a full-time maid, not a part-time housekeeper."

"But Mrs. Benson does a wonderful job—"

"Yes, I know. When she's here. But that's only twice a week. I guess I'm lucky to have her at all though. It's so hard to find anyone to come to the house and clean anymore. Becca, I want you to make a list for me. We must get everything ready—Becca!"

The girl wrenched her mind away from the wonderful idea that had just occurred to her. "Oh—yeah. A list. I gotcha."

Mrs. Carraway tutted impatiently. "Really, Becca. Please watch your language. Do you want Joshua to grow up talking like that?"

* * *

The plane arrived five minutes early. Cathy examined the map from the rental car agency, her route marked clearly in yellow highlighter. She set out for McLeod.

It was not hard to find. Directional signs to historic McLeod dotted the freeway. Cathy felt certain she could find it without a map.

The campus, a mix of frame and red brick buildings, charmed her at first sight. She parked near the administration building as Donovan had instructed in his telefax.

Getting out of the car, she settled her shades firmly on her nose and headed towards the designated building.

Cathy was glad she'd worn a simple trouser suit for travel. She discarded the jacket the moment she felt the warmer Georgia air. Her silk blouse kept her professional look intact, but it also felt light and cool against her skin.

At the door, she took a deep breath and went inside. She stopped in awe.

Until then, Cathy did not know what she had expected. She knew it wasn't this gigantic wall of history, where mammoth portraits of educators hung side by side the length of the hallway.

She saw Mary McLeod Bethune, W.E.B. DuBois, and Booker T. Washington. She whirled to face Marva Collins, Mary Berry, and John Blassingame. There were educators from McLeod's past, their names neatly chronicled in gold plates under their portraits. She turned back to the other room—and collided with a woman coming out of another door.

Folders of papers scattered across the gleaming wood floor.

"Oh goodness, I am so sorry," Cathy apologized, but the woman was already bending down to gather her files.

"You should watch where you're going young lady!" she snapped.

"I'm sorry," Cathy apologized again. "Here let me help you."

"Don't step on anything!" the woman ordered.

Cathy bent down, carefully gathering the papers. As she did, the cuff of her blouse rose, revealing the slim gold watch. She was late for her interview.

"Oh, hell," she muttered, straightening herself back up. "Here." She thrust the papers at the woman. "I'm sorry, but I really must go."

"But, my papers—you young folks—"

"I'm sorry," Cathy called.

"Inconsiderate students," the woman muttered.

* * *

Chris gave Belle a telling look as she hurried past into Donovan's office.

"I know. I know." Belle whispered, handing her a stack of crumpled papers and folders. "Could you put these in order for me? Thanks."

She gave a quick knock and dived into Donovan's office.

"Sorry I'm late," she told the group, "but this kid practically plowed over me and knocked a thousand papers out of my hands without helping to pick them up."

"That's okay, Belle. Professor Carraway was a few minutes late herself. We were just about to get started."

In her haste, Belle had not noticed the other occupants in the room. She quickly searched for the stranger, seeing Mark's tight face an instant before landing on the pretty, trim girl from the hallway.

"You—you aren't—"

"I was just getting to introductions," Donovan boomed proudly. "Everyone, this is Dr. Catherine Carraway."

* * *

Monday, Becca raised her new idea with her father-in-law as they worked on the timesheets for Friday's payroll.

"I don't know, Becca. We've been doing fine with just commercial contracting."

"I know, but this here's a chance to change things up a little. I hear it from the women at the spa all the time. They don't have time to cook and clean and do laundry, or they're worn out from doing it all."

"So, why don't they hire somebody?"

"They don't have time to do the looking or they don't know how to go about it. That's where we'd come in."

"I don't know—"

"Look. Just like now, if a developer or a building manager needs something cleaned, they know to call us. It's the same thing."

"But, we go into places after everyone else goes home."

"The hours are different," she conceded, "and I wouldn't use the same people anyway. We need a couple or three girls for this. Maybe even college girls who need extra money."

"And if something goes missing or gets broken?"

"We bond 'em the same as we bond employees right now."

"I don't know—"

"I'll pay 'em myself," Becca interrupted. "Please, Mr. Carraway. I know this can work."

Robert tried to remember the last time Becca had asked for anything, and couldn't. "Okay," he agreed. "We'll try it. For one quarter. And you don't have to pay them anything. We can afford to at least try your idea."

* * *

Belle saw his car in her headlights as she drove up the drive to her house.

"Donovan," she called to the man on the porch. "Been waitin' long?"

He shook his head. "The nurse said you'd just gone down to the store."

Belle came up the porch steps with a small bag. "Daddy's weakness: zero bars."

"I kinda like that white chocolate myself."

"And to what do I owe this rare visit? Or should I guess?"

Donovan cleared his throat. "I wanted to talk to you about Catherine Carraway."

"You want to hire her, you mean."

"I'd like your support, Belle."

"Pam is the best candidate."

"For your job or for Congress? Belle, she's gonna run for office, and you know it. And she can't run the campaign from McLeod."

"Grace?"

"I know the woman isn't qualified and so do you. Be honest Belle. You didn't want Catherine Carraway because you thought she was white. What could you possibly have against her now that you know she's black?"

"— Hell, she probably doesn't even think she's black. Sho' don't sound like it. And, she's young."

"She'd be the youngest on the faculty, but that's not a bad thing. Maybe too many of us are getting old."

"She don't know nothing 'bout these kids."

"What's there to know about any student these days? They all dress funny and listen to MTV."

"She's arrogant and rude—"

"Yeah," Donovan agreed. "Kinda put me in the mind of you a few years ago."

"God." Belle stumped away into the house, the door slamming behind her.

"Was that a 'yes' or a 'no'?" Donovan laughed. He laughed all the way home.

* * *

Becca and Josh sat at the dining room table. They could hear "Wheel of Fortune" from the living room.

"Is this a good picture, mommy?"

Becca looked up from the business plan she was writing for "Maid to Order."

"It's a beautiful picture, honey. Can I have it for my collection?"

* * *

Cathy was excited. She was about to embark on a new adventure. The dean expressed a flattering amount of disappointment at losing her. A group of her colleagues arranged a farewell party, where they all talked about their own plans for leaving and drank too much.

On the drive to the South, she mused about how her mother had been tight-lipped with disapproval. When Cathy suggested that her parents might like to visit, Virginia responded that they had no reason ever to step foot in the state of Georgia. Though her father frowned, he did not contradict his wife. Cathy drove on, determined not to let her parents rattle her. She comforted herself thinking about how excited and happy both Becca and Rob were about her new title—Distinguished Professor of English and Literature. She was surprised her mother wasn't bowled over as well. Changing jobs should be a routine matter, she thought. Since downsizing began in the eighties, people changed jobs every few years. The emergence of the global economy forced people to move to different countries for their careers all the time. They went from Tennessee to Thailand, from Boise to Beijing. She was only moving a few states away. And although the time zone was different, there was no ocean to cross, no foreign language and customs to learn. It was the unseasonably warm day that was causing the sticky perspiration in her armpits and the small of her back. Fear and worry played no part at all.

* * *

Cathy settled quickly into the small town. There was little rental property in the area. With Mark's help, she bought four acres of land and installed a modular home onto it. If she couldn't sell it when she left McLeod, she could keep it as a vacation home.

She encountered Belle at the local market one day. Although Cathy smiled, the older woman looked right through her.

* * *

The late bell rang for the first class on the first day of the new semester at McLeod. Cathy smiled nervously at the group of young faces and introduced herself.

"This is the syllabus we'll be following this semester." She handed a stack to a nearby student who passed them on. "I stick to it, so I expect you to do the same. Due dates are never moved," she warned. "Any questions?"

No one had questions. She launched into the lecture she had prepared.

* * *

Mark stuck his head into Cathy's office. "Wanna have dinner tonight?" he asked. Despite his disappointment that Cathy was not who he thought, the two still became friends.

"Can't." She grimaced at the stack in front of her. "Papers to grade."

"Some other time, then?"

"Sure. Goodnight, Mark."

Nearly two hours later, Cathy put aside the last paper from her first class. She frowned at the stack. Not one reflected any originality. Not one offered any challenge to points raised by her lectures. On every page, paper after paper, she heard her own voice.

She reached for the second stack. She didn't stop until she had read papers from all her classes. They all sounded like her. Where were the voices of her students?

* * *

Belle looked at the clock. It was five a.m. She grabbed the phone before the ringing could wake her father.

"Hello."

"Hello, Labelle. How are you?"

"Stephon," she sighed. "Don't you ever look at a clock before you call?"

"Ah, I forget the time difference, didn't I? I apologize. I wanted to inquire about your father. He is better, yes?"

"Much better, thanks. He's almost back to his old self. El nouveau."

"So, he could travel to visit family, no?"

"You aren't family anymore, Stephon." She repeated it in French.

"We were married in the church, Labelle. In the eyes of God, it will always be so."

"Papa's not up to traveling to France. He's not doing *that* much better. Besides, you know he hates to fly."

"You would not lie to me, cherie?"

"No."

"Then I must wait to have the pleasure of your company."

"You could always come here for a visit."

"Always, it is the same problem with us, eh my belle. You cannot bear to leave your lovely McLeod, and I cannot part myself from home here."

"I'll let Dad know you called," she promised and hung up. Stephon was still pretentious. All of the Macheau's were, as far as Belle was concerned. But deep in her heart she knew she still loved him. Sometimes she asked herself if she was being unfair in designating Stephon's French accent as being fake. After all, he was born in France. But, no. Stephon's foreign intonation wasn't the reason they were not compatible. She wasn't cut out for marriage, especially one that spanned an ocean. She was too committed to her students at McLeod.

* * *

Cathy felt the air leave the tire the moment she hit the rock. She braked carefully and looked at the gash.

The last thing she needed was a flat tire. She was miles from her house. There was no water left in the bottle attached to the handlebars. And now she had to walk all the way home on a hot summer morning—she calculated four miles.

She put down the kick-stand and walked carefully over the ground. She had not hit a rock after all, but a large, jagged piece of glass from a Coke bottle.

She carefully picked up the glass and put it in her fanny pack. She'd throw it away when she got home.

A half hour later, she wondered. Could she make it home? She was hot, tired, and angry. And her feet hurt.

"Ain't ya 'posed to ride 'stead of push?" a gravelly voice called from the shade ahead.

Her discomfort had distracted Cathy enough for her to miss the old man walking slowly towards her.

"I've got a flat tire," she explained.

"Dat'll do it," he said, turning to walk in her direction. "Ya got far?"

"About three maybe four miles. I live near the old Williard farm."

"Ya Dr. Carraway from da college?"

"Yes sir."

"Thought so. I know most everyone from 'round here."

Cathy smiled. The man certainly looked old enough to know everyone. "Who are you?"

"Folk calls me old Geral'. They usted call me youn' Geral' 'cause my daddy, he was old Geral'."

"It's nice meeting you, Mr. Gerald."

"My place just up the road a piece. Sorry ma girl ain't home. She coulda run you home in no time."

"I don't mind," Cathy smiled. "I wanted exercise."

"Ya shore getting it, 'den. But I's got to tell ya. You shouldn't be out alone."

Cathy shrugged. "I never see anyone."

"They's wild dogs," he warned. "Ya got a stick or some'um wid ya?"

She shook her head. "I guess I could always climb a tree."

Old Geral' cast his watery eyes doubtfully over her spandex outfit. "Best git yoself a big stick instead," he advised, and Cathy laughed.

She encountered him again a few days later. She stopped the bike, with its new tire, and walked with him for a few minutes. She enjoyed his humor and the stories he told about the area and its people.

"You ought to write a book," Cathy told him one day, about a month later. Encountering Old Gerald had become part of her routine. She started spending a few minutes listening to him out of kindness. Now, she looked forward to seeing the old man. One day, he brought her a hefty stick. Mostly, they told each other stories. Today, he'd shared a gripping civil war story.

"Too old," he declared. "Sides, ma girl's da smart one in da family. Ya outta come by da house and say how-do one day."

"I'd like that," Cathy said. She looked at her watch. She was always careful not to keep the old man too long in the growing heat. "I'd better finish my ride before it gets too hot. See you tomorrow, Gerald."

* * *

Becca read the letter twice, then folded and returned it to the envelope. She left the kitchen and went quietly into the living room. She waited for Tom Brokaw to stop for a commerical break.

"Mr. and Mrs. Carraway?"

"Yes, dear?" Virginia asked.

"I got a letter from Rob today. It say he'll be home for Christmas for sure."

"Rob! Rob's coming home?"

"Yes ma'am. At least three weeks, he think."

"Robert? Robert, did you hear that?"

"You almost burst my eardrum with the news."

"We have got to plan something extra special. A party, perhaps, with some of his best friends from high school and college. Rob always knew so many people ..."

Becca slipped away as Mrs. Carraway continued to make plans.

* * *

The students filed into the classroom. Cathy, dressed simply in a cotton jumper, smiled at each one. Some returned the smile tentatively.

"Good morning," she told the room as the last student took a seat. "My name is Cathy Carraway. I'm your English Lit teacher for the semester. Before we get into the syllabus and assignments, I want to go around the room and have each of you introduce yourselves. Tell us your name, where you're from, why you chose McLeod, and what you like most to read..."

* * *

"You are kidding me?" Mark Simmons said as he put a piece of pecan pie on his tray. They had driven to a K&W restaurant near Atlanta for dinner. "You actually let them choose the reading list?"

"I gave them a list and I let them vote on the top ten," Cathy admitted.

"I don't know about that."

"It's their time and energy." Cathy paid the cashier. "They ought to spend it on what interests them the most."

"I just don't think it's a good idea to give students that kind of control."

"The inmates running the asylum, hum?" Cathy teased.

"It's not funny," Mark corrected her sternly. "As educators, it's our responsibility to set the highest standards necessary to stimulate and challenge the young minds in our classrooms."

"I agree." She savored a strawberry in her fruit salad. "I just gave them a choice of stimuli, that's all."

* * *

"Got a minute?" Donovan pulled Belle aside one day near Thanksgiving when she came by the Administration Building to pick up her paycheck and check her mail.

"I want to show you something," he drew her into his office.

"You look a bit tired," she said, concerned. "I hope you're planning to get some rest over the break."

"Janet insists. In fact, she keeps nagging me to retire and take up something else part-time."

"Your wife's a smart woman. I always did like her."

"Here they are. Don't worry. They're photocopies. Feel free to take them home and let me know what you think later. I want your opinion on this."

Belle returned them after the holiday. "They're wonderful," she reported. "The themes are very well developed, the styles are distinct, personal, and interesting. They were all good, but two of the five were simply excellent. Are these from a student interested in our grad program?"

"Not exactly," Donovan said, pouring water into a poinsettia. "They may want to go to graduate school one day, but right now, they're in Cathy Carraway's freshman English class."

* * *

Cathy didn't see Gerald until she was on the return leg of her bicycle ride. Like her, he was headed for home.

"Good morning. I thought you'd decided to give today a miss."

"Overslept. Dis nu medication don't agree wid me yet."

"You haven't been over-doing it?" she asked, as they came to his driveway.

"My daughter, she don't lemme do nothin', much less ovado."

A screen door slammed. "Papa? Papa?"

"Lordy lord," Gerald declared under his breath. "She done caught me."

"You mean you're not supposed to be out here?" Cathy whispered back guiltily.

"I needed to stretch ma legs. A man can't stretch his legs?"

"Maybe I should go with you and apologize for keeping you."

"You can come and meet my daughter, but you got no cause to 'pologize for nothin'."

Cathy pushed the bike slowly up the drive, her steps measured to pace her escort.

"Ya still goin' home for Christmas?"

"Got my ticket in the mail yesterday."

"Papa!"

"I'm coming, woman!" he called. "Can't you see I got a pretty girl wid me?"

Cathy looked up, laughter in her eyes. It disappeared when she met the cold stare of Old Gerald's daughter, Belle Williams.

* * *

The entire family waited in the terminal as the passengers from Rob's plane disembarked. The holiday packed the airport with travelers.

Cathy saw him first, and he gave her a broad smile and waved. Then he looked past her, his eyes searching until a look of utter joy came over his face. Cathy followed his gaze and realized that her brother had found Becca's face in the crowd.

* * *

Belle and her father sat on the porch. Each drank whiskey, although Old Gerald's glass had more water than liquor. A car drove by with the radio blasting the sounds of the rapper Tupac.

"It's a wonda it don't break they ears. It shore hurt mine."

"Come on, papa. It's not that bad."

"You like that there rap music, Belle honey? Don't tell me you be playing it after I go to bed."

"No," she laughed softly, "but I don't dismiss it neither. It's really no different from da Negro spirituals dat protested slavery, or da rock music dat protested the war in Vietnam. Maybe mo' vulgar—"

"Ya telling me," her father agreed.

"Even Shakespeare referred to women as 'harlots,' papa, and there are similar references in da Bible dat amount to women being called 'whores'—"

"Ya watcha mouth there, girl," he ordered. "Ya moma and me didn't raise you to talk like that."

"Sorry papa," Belle soothed. "I'm just saying dat their profane use of language may stem from da deeper, mo' personal rage of where dese kids come from. Gangs, drive-by shootings, being lucky to live past yo' teens—with dat depth of suffering on dey young shoulders, how can dey not be mo' angry than hippies against some war an ocean away?"

"Next you gonna tell me ya gonna teach da kids rap music."

"Well, most of it does conform to an a-b-a-b rhyme scheme," she joked.

* * *

"Boris Yeltsin is getting just what he deserves," Cathy argued over dinner. "He undermined Gorbachev. Now he sees for himself: it's a heck of a lot easier to throw stones from the sidelines than to rule."

"The Russian people see him as a modern day George Washington," Rob said.

"George Washington?" Joshua piped up. "Momma told me he was the first president of the United States, didn't you momma?"

"Yes sweetie," Becca said shyly as Rob winked at her.

"Your mom's one smart lady," he told his son. "And good-looking too."

"Rob," his mother cut in, "you are too thin. You must have some more turkey and dressing. And tell us, what do you think about the Labor chances in England? I heard a report that even Margaret Thatcher has no confidence in John Major."

And, as at countless other meals, the Carraway family spoke of world events and little else.

* * *

The kettle whistled, and Cathy quickly removed it from the stove to make her hot tea. It was the middle of the night, but her internal clock was too messed up for her to sleep.

She took her tea into the den. Putting a log onto the fire, she sat cross-legged in front of the fireplace. Rows of cards adorned the mantle. Curious, she rose to examine them.

She recognized the names of her father's employees and members from her family church. There were also a few cards from banks and other firms that did business with her father.

Each card expressed a warm sentiment regarding family and the holidays. Yet they were all different. She wondered what her mother must think about that. One of the cards even featured a black Santa Claus saying "Yo, Yo, Yo." Certainly Virginia must not have noticed. Cathy smiled to herself and finished her tea.

* * *

Mark Simmons snapped his fingers to get Chris' attention.

"Is Donovan available?" he demanded when the woman finally looked up from her computer. "I need to speak with him."

"I'm sorry, but the Chair is in an important meeting and can't be disturbed."

"Really? Who's in with him?"

"Belle, of course." Chris smiled smugly. "They meet about once a week, you know?"

* * *

Cathy smiled at Brandon Edwards, who was struggling in her English Literature class.

"Your poem can address anything you want. This module is on themes in American literature."

"That's the problem, Dr. Carraway. Maybe it's too broad for me. Can you narrow it down to something?"

"You narrow it yourself. No one has to agree with you, Brandon. This is about your perspective." As the student still looked worried, she added, "Look, which of the writers that we've studied so far have you liked the best?"

Brandon concentrated for a moment. "I guess that would be Stephen Crane's *Once I Saw Mountains Angry*. I kinda liked the way he talked about one man prevailing against the odds. But, "he added with more excitement, "I really liked Robinson's *Richard Cory*. The isolation of classism, the corrupting impact of money. But maybe that's because you played us the song. It kinda moved me, you know?"

"The lyrics of a song can be a form of poetic expression."

"I don't know Dr. Carraway. I mean, I know what I want to say, but when I think of how to say it, it's like my mind goes blank."

"What would you say to your friends?"

"Huh?"

"If you were hanging out with friends, what would you say to them?"

"I can write it like that?"

"Yes. Language is a tool for self-expression, Brandon. Use it in any way to express your perspective. Write it the way it would move you. Give value to your language and dialect. It's okay."

* * *

Belle came into the kitchen and sniffed the air with heartfelt pleasure. She had been to a symposium in Boston and the smells of home delighted her.

"Is that banana nut bread? Papa, don't tell me you went and cooked my favorite?"

Old Gerald offered her a sample. "Whacha think?"

She took small bits, savoring the smooth texture and nutty flavor. "Heaven," she declared. "But, papa, you don't need to be working in a hot kitchen—"

"Don't worry. I didn't."

"You got the nurse—"

"Nope."

"Then—no. It's too good to be store-brought."

"Didn't get it from no sto'. Got it from dat girl's that's always riding her bike up and down da road."

Belle nearly choked. "Cathy Carraway?"

"Yep. 'Course, I gave her da recipe, but she didn't mess it up too much."

* * *

Becca was examining a delivery of cleaning supplies when Sophie burst into the storage room.

"Becca! Becca, you'd better come quick. It's Mr. Carraway."

Becca dropped the clipboard and ran towards the office. She found her father-in-law in the grips of a seizure. "Call 9-1-1," she ordered. Sophie went to the phone.

"Don't worry, Mr. Carraway. Everything is okay." She spoke gently, thankful for the CPR course she'd taken at the local YMCA a few years back. Becca loosened his tie and the buttons on his shirt and repositioned him on the sofa. She kept up a soothing dialogue until the paramedics arrived to take Mr. Carraway to the hospital.

* * *

"You're a lucky man," the doctor told Mr. Carraway a short time later. He smiled at Becca, who was standing with Mrs. Carraway in a private room. "If you have a heart attack, it's good to have someone who knows CPR handy. Although your attack was mild, we want to keep you here for a few days to run some tests."

"What do you mean by a few days?"

"Two or three at the most."

Virginia, who had been squeezing Robert's hand, asked, "He's been working too hard, hasn't he? He's been expanding the company. I told him it was a bad idea. "She glared at Becca.

"The body does need to rest, but it needs activity too. Is there a history of heart disease in the family?"

"I seem to remember my mother's father—when he died, they said it was heart trouble. But I don't really know."

"We'll know more after the tests. You might have to watch your diet more carefully and get more exercise. But don't worry about that now. Your family can visit for a few more minutes. After that, I want you to relax and get some sleep. We'll be doing some of the tests in the middle of the night."

"This is your fault," Virginia accused Becca as soon as the door closed.

"Ginny, that is not true," Robert shot back. "If anything, Becca's been keeping it from happening sooner. And you heard what the doctor said. It was a good thing she was there today."

"If she wasn't there, it wouldn't have happened at all. All these grand notions of expansion. She's not a business woman."

"Becca's a hell of a business woman, Ginny. Her idea for the maid service increased our business by twenty percent and it's still climbing."

"Humph—"

"You owe her an apology."

"Oh, Mr. Carraway, that's okay," Becca put in, but they ignored her.

"Ginny," he warned.

"Well, sure I'm sorry if I offended anybody."

"You call that an apology? You can do better."

"Robert, you can't be serious," she hissed.

"I won't be able to rest until you've apologized to that girl. Ginny, she's borne the sharp edge of your tongue year after year without a whimper. God knows why. Maybe I should've said something before, but I definitely will not lie in this hospital bed and have you wrongly accuse her of putting me in it. She's been a tremendous help to me in the business, and I know she'll do a good job running it while I'm laid up. Now apologize to her, Ginny. Right now."

Virginia looked at the man who had been her husband for nearly forty years. She straightened her shoulders, turned to Becca, and said,

"Please accept my apology, Becca. I'm afraid all of this has upset me terribly. Of course, I thank you for your assistance. We all do."

"No problem," Becca said. "I mean, sure. You're welcome."

* * *

A rhythmic clap surprised Belle as she walked down the hall of the English building during the spring semester. She followed the noise to a classroom. She paused at the door and peeped inside. A student stood at the front of the room of clapping students. As she watched, he broke out into a rap:

> "It's hard on a brother
> Born into a society
> Of low expectations
> Of what he's gonna be.
>
> Try as he might
> It's a losing fight
> To make people see
> A different reality.
>
> They say, you can't be this
> You can't do that.
> When they really mean
> They won't let
>
> You reach your potential
> Strive for your dream—"

"What in the world!"

Belle jumped, startled by Mark's bark of outrage from behind her.

"Shh," she urged as he came up to peer through the pane.

"I can't believe this!" he whispered, still indignant. "Is that student rapping? What in the world is Cathy thinking?"

"Maybe Dr. Carraway's using it to teach iambic pentameters," Belle suggested, dead-pan.

"She can't do that!" he declared. "Can she?"

Belle shrugged. "You wanted age diversity," she reminded him and moved on.

*　*　*

Old Gerald eyed the huge box skeptically.

"Happy Birthday," Cathy said.

"What is it?"

She shook her head. "Open it and find out."

His firm hands ripped the bright-colored paper off as quickly as Joshua would have.

"A bicycle?" he said. "You kiddin'?"

"Don't tell me you never rode one?"

"Maybe fifty, sixty year ago."

"They say you never forget."

"Humph."

"Just try it," she coaxed. "I thought you might keep me company sometimes."

"Den ya should've got me a big stick to go wid da bike."

*　*　*

Josh and Becca came for a week with Mr. Carraway to visit Cathy.

"He misses you," Becca said when Cathy came to the porch after putting Josh to bed. "Even more than he misses his father. He almost never sees Rob. But you've always been there for him."

"It's good to see you both," Cathy said. "And Dad looks so much better. He says he's semi-retired now."

"Yeah." They both looked to where Mr. Carraway was weeding Cathy's small vegetable garden. "He only comes into the office three days a week, and even then, we don't let him do nothing."

"He must love that."

"Oh, he complains, but it's best for him. He's done his part. He shouldn't have to work so hard now. Matter of fact, Rob figures he'll get out this next tour."

"Really?"

"Yeah. He knows he's needed at home. And he don't like the idea of being a skranger to his son."

"It'll be good to have him home," Cathy said.

Becca grinned.

"What?" Cathy said.

"You said 'home', like you still think of Madison and not here."
"Oh."
"Does that mean you coming back? It's been a couple years."
"I don't know. Maybe. But not yet."

* * *

Cathy mused at the pictures of Rob and Becca's new house. She made a mental note to call Joshua and thank him for the crayon rendering of the house.

She put the pictures aside as she began grading another stack of papers. She was one-third of the way through when a passage in a student's paper struck a familiar chord. She looked at the graded papers. No, the memory it recalled was more distant. She read on. Has she seen this style of writing before? She flipped to the cover page. Reading the name, she understood why the prose was familiar.

* * *

Melissa Jones smiled as she entered Cathy's office. The smile faded when she saw her brother, Roger, already seated.
"You wanted to see me, Dr. Carraway?"
"Come on in, Melissa."

* * *

Mark Simmons parked in the faculty lot, surprised to see Cathy's car already there at seven. He went into the building, knocked on her door, and opened it.
"They say the early bird catches the worm," he quoted, then stopped when he saw she was not alone.
"Let's finish this debate another time, okay?"
The young man lifted his large frame quickly, moving with the speed that made him an All-American.
"Peace," he said. Books in one hand, he went to the door. Mark stepped aside for him to pass.
"Wasn't that our star running back?" he asked, looking down the hall.
"Uh-huh," Cathy answered absently, clearing her desk.
"But he's not one of your students?"

"No." She closed a drawer.
"So? What's up? What was he doing here?"
"Excuse me?"
"Roger Jones. Why was he here?"
"Oh. He was returning some research materials."
"At this hour?"
"Why not? You're here, aren't you? Was there something you wanted? I need to make some photocopies before my eight o'clock class."

* * *

People of all ages packed the room as a panel debated the merits of rap music. Cathy wondered again why she had accepted the invitation. As one of the organizers, Grace Wavell obviously had stacked the audience with her supporters. The other panelists, who had expressed support for rap music, had been intimidated into silence by the crowd.

"I'd like to ask Ms. Wavell, how much rap music have you listened to?"

"Almost everything that's been recorded. For my book, *Giving Music a Bad Rap*, I specifically dealt with the period between 1987, when the first rap song sold a million copies, and 1995."

"And how many drive-by shootings have you participated in?" Cathy asked.

"What?"

"Sold any crack lately?" Cathy continued. "Shaken your booty? Joined the Crips?"

"Of course not," Grace protested.

"Why not?" Cathy demanded. "If rap music is responsible for violence and moral decay, as you claim, then surely its evil influence has gripped someone who has exposed herself to as much rap as you have."

"That's absurd. This isn't about me. I'm a mature adult—"

"And so are most of the people who buy rap music." Cathy looked directly at the audience. "I apologize for asking Ms. Wavell about her personal activities. I know she's not a gang member or a drug trafficker. She's a hard-working professional, just like the majority of the music-buying public. I hope you all will forgive the sarcasm I used to make the point about the misconceptions behind rap. The truth is, it's easy to lead the masses to frenzy by highlighting the most offensive, anti-social phrases in rap music."

"And they are there. But we should never lose sight of the fact that rap music is just a medium. Rap music doesn't kill. It doesn't sell crack cocaine. We had murders and drugs long before rap came on the scene—in fact, long before Thomas Edison invented the record player."

"It is easy to blame the medium. A date took me to see "Silence of the Lambs." It's about a man who likes to murder people and then eat them. Believe me, the movie did not make me want to become a cannibal. Yet, if we are to believe Ms. Wavell, I should be sizing you all up for my next meal. Don't worry. You're safe."

"Let's say, for the sake of harmony, that I did agree with Ms. Wavell about the awful influence of some rap music. Then I would have to be truthful and point out that rap represents less than one percent of all record sales. I would have to be truthful and ask, do you know what most songs are about? Love. Overwhelmingly, the songs in the Top Forty during the last fifty years have been about love. A few have actually been religious spirituals. Do we credit these songs and these musicians with making the world a better place? Has Barry Manilow, Elton John, Whitney Houston, or Garth Brooks—the artists who have been the most successful worldwide since the 1970s—ever gotten a Nobel Peace Prize?"

"You're mixing apples and oranges," Grace shouted over the scattered applause. "If you read my book—"

"I did read your book. In fact, I had my entire freshman English class at McLeod read your book, and we listened to every rap song you criticized. "Cathy shook her head. "I hate to report that not one student committed a violent act as a result. But then, McLeod students, who are exceptional, to start with, may be the exceptions to Ms. Wavell's 'Rap Rules', which are listed in her new book."

"Critics of rap are much like critics of all media. Like us, they want to blame something controllable. Things, after all, are more controllable than people. In trying to answer the age-old question of why people do bad things, we fall into the trap of blaming modern inventions. We blame TV, music, movies. We hate to admit the truth: people make bad decisions and do bad things. Some people are just plain evil or crazy. They do bad things for reasons as simple as jealousy, greed, boredom. That truth has been with us since Cain killed Abel."

* * *

Belle greeted Chris with a tired smile when she arrived. When Dr. Donovan Burke had retired after his silver anniversary at McLeod College, no one was surprised that Belle Williams had succeeded him as chairperson of the English Department.

"Great," Chris said. "You're here."

"Is something wrong?"

"The phone's ringing off the hook. You've got a dozen messages."

"What's going on?"

"Dr. Carraway," Chris stated, as though the two words explained. "Universities are calling to offer her speaking engagements, the ACLU and other First Amendment groups are calling to interview her, the 'Today Show' wants her to appear live—" The phone interrupted her. Another line began ringing. "See. What do I do?"

"Does Dr. Carraway have an answering machine in her office?"

"No."

"Then keep taking messages. I'll unplug mine. Find a fresh tape and take it all up to her office. Then transfer her calls. We're not her publicity service."

* * *

"We saw you on TV," Rob told her during their weekly call. "Josh was quite the celebrity at school. And mom! She's got a zillion tapes."

"I can't believe this is getting so much attention," Cathy protested. "I published a perfectly good paper last year on symbolism in black literature. I covered more than a century of published works. No one ever asks about that."

"Is it true that there's going to be a rapper's salute to you at the Grammys? Becca saw it on the front page of one of those supermarket tabloids."

"This is crazy. I'm hanging up now. Give my love to everyone."

* * *

Old Gerald was waiting for her the next evening.

"Sorry 'bout dis. I was out on dat contrapshun and got too tired to go back."

"That's okay. Do you need some water?"

"Just needed a rest. I should be gitting on back now."

"Get in the car while I throw your bike in the trunk."

"You've been busy," Gerald commented on the drive home.

"A bit," Cathy admitted, still embarrassed by all the attention. She hated to consider what Belle must be thinking now that she was department Chair. She knew Grace Wavell was a friend of Belle's. She hoped there would not be a confrontation when she took Gerald home. She enjoyed her friendship with Belle's father, but she had yet to gain any ground with Belle herself.

Two cars were parked in the driveway.

"You've got company," Cathy said.

"Probably the sheriff," he muttered.

"In a Caddy?"

Gerald sighed. "You best come in."

Cathy propped the bike against the porch and followed Gerald inside.

"There you are, papa," Belle greeted them. She acknowledged Cathy with a curt nod. "I was getting worried. Did you forget Pam and her son were coming to dinner?"

"I got a bit tired. Cathy gave me a ride back."

"That was nice of you, Dr. Carraway," Belle said stiffly.

"It was no problem. I'd best be going myself—"

"Belle, surely this isn't the young woman we've seen so much on television lately?"

"Congresswoman Pam Avery, Dr. Carraway."

The two women shook hands.

"David?" She called her son. "Come meet Dr. Carraway. The new darling of the media."

"I don't know about that," Cathy demurred as she shook hands with David Avery.

"Of course you are," Pam declared. "I was just telling Belle how much I wanted to meet you."

Belle gave her dad an ironic look. "And suddenly, here she is."

"I'd just love to have you as the speech writer for my next campaign," Pam drew her into the dining room. "You'll stay for dinner, of course. Belle, you'll set another place, won't you? A good Southern hostess always has room for one more at her table. Gerald, you look as handsome as ever. I insist you sit beside me."

* * *

Belle stood with Cathy and her father as the lights of the Cadillac disappeared onto the main road.

Cathy thought she had never met anyone so forceful. She didn't realize she'd spoken her thoughts aloud until Belle agreed.

"Pam wants what she wants. Let's have coffee in the den," she said.

"It was a lovely dinner," Cathy began to decline politely.

"You'll like the coffee, too. Papa, you don't mind if I talk to your riding buddy a few minutes, do you?"

"Seems Cathy's da one ya oughtta ax. I'm putting my bones to bed. 'Night."

"Make yourself comfortable," Belle told Cathy as she flipped on the den light. "I'll be right back with the coffee."

Cathy perched nervously on the edge of a wing chair, wondering how she had ever gotten into this situation. At least she'd met David as a result.

"It's decaffeinated," Belle entered the room with a tray.

"That's fine."

"I wanted to tell you that you shouldn't let Pam pressure you into something you don't want to do. You probably figured out that she sent Papa to fetch you tonight."

"I did wonder," Cathy admitted.

"She's sincere, and if you are interested in working for her campaign, no one at McLeod will stand in your way."

"I'm not sure I'm suited to the political arena. I prefer teaching."

"McLeod is lucky to have you." Belle drained her cup. "You seem surprised."

"It's just that you've never said anything like that to me before."

"You weren't my choice," Belle said bluntly, "but, it's been over a year. I think it's time to admit I may have been wrong."

Cathy pressed. "May have been?"

Belle shrugged. "I also wanted to mention an interesting letter I got the other day." She rose and went to her desk. She handed a sheet of paper to Cathy. "Know anything about it?"

Cathy looked at the letterhead of a well-known Atlanta law firm. The letter was succinct, and she had no doubts that it was legal.

"I had no idea," Cathy said.

"It seems their client, Roger Jones, received special tutoring from someone here at McLeod. Tutoring that helped him deal with dyslexia some of his previous schools never caught because they were too busy passing him so he could play football. I don't think he's given them the same kind of contribution he sent McLeod. He contributed here because you took the time to help him."

Cathy shook her head. "If his sister hadn't been in my class, too, I might never have found out either."

"But you did, Dr. Carraway."

"I'm thrilled for the school, of course. I guess I never knew football paid so much."

"That's probably just some of his shoe money from commercials."

"Wow."

* * *

Congresswoman Avery called the next morning. Cathy politely but firmly declined her job offer. She did recommend a former student whom she felt Pam should consider.

David Avery called a few hours later.

"Can I take you to dinner?" he asked.

Cathy didn't turn him down.

* * *

Belle recalled the first time she had heard the woman's clear, standard English. She laughed out loud when she remembered their first meeting. She really had disliked the woman. She sounded so … white. Now here she was nurturing the students and bringing more money to McLeod than Belle ever had. Stephon had told her countless times not to judge a book by its cover. She was so wrapped up in language. She turned her thoughts to Stephon next.

* * *

It has been a long time, but Cathy knew this feeling. Her heart raced every time she thought about him. She replayed each date upon returning home in the evenings. She was caught up in a whirlwind of happiness. Cathy was in love.

* * *

"A Congresswoman's son," Virginia Carraway beamed as she helped her daughter pack. "I knew moving to Georgia was just what you needed."

Cathy and David had flown to Madison for the wedding. In a burst of sentimentality, she had wanted her father to give her in marriage at her childhood church. Now, the couple was flying to Hawaii for a weeklong honeymoon.

"David's a teacher like me, mother," she warned. "He doesn't have political aspirations. We'll both be teaching at McLeod next year."

"You never know," Virginia pronounced as though she did. "What in the world? Did you pack this by mistake?"

"This" was a plain brown package that Gerald had given her before she left Georgia.

Virginia held it delicately by the tips of her fingers.

"Don't open it 'til after the wedding," he said. She had wanted him there, but he'd refused to fly.

She took the small package from her mother and gently removed the tape.

It was a book, a hardcover edition of Labelle Macheau's new novel, *Between the Thunder*.

"A bit inexpensive for a wedding gift isn't it?" Virginia sniffed.

Cathy ignored her and flipped open the cover. A card, written in Old Gerald's rolling cursive, fell to the floor. Cathy picked it up and read, "I know she's your favorite. I made her autograph it specially."

"Gerald, what in the world have you done?" Cathy whispered to her absent friend. Carefully, she flipped open the cover again. And caught her breath at what she read:

"To my father's dear friend, and riding buddy. With best wishes, Belle Williams."

"Gracious, dear," Virginia declared. "What are you crying for? It may be cheap, but it's the thought that counts, isn't it?"

* * *

In Language and Symbolic Power, Bourdieu says "if linguistic theories have tended to neglect the social-historical conditions underlying the formation of the language which they take, in an idealized form, as their object domain, so too they have tended to analyze linguistic expressions in isolation from the specific social conditions in which they are used." (Page 7). In applying Bourdieu's evaluation to the characters in The Words Unspoken, one can see how each character's social background has been instrumental in how they speak:

Cathy Carraway

"So, what are we really talking about when we talk about language? How should we define it? Should we be talking about the spoken word or the unspoken?" Cathy Carraway asks her students. Cathy continues "often, the language we use fits our goals at the time. We have 'lines' for every situation, don't we? Hang out at the Quad," she named a popular college club, "and you'll hear all kinds of lines, especially around closing time when people don't want to go home alone." "There is a language for romance, a language for business, a language we use in religion."

The character Cathy Carraway is a study in Golden's (1959) philosophy[1] that "standard language is the key that will open many doors, and conversely, many doors may be closed to those with non-stan-

---

1. Golden, R.I. Improving Patterns of Language Usage, Detroit: Wayne State University Press, 1959.

dard language." At her mother's insistence, Cathy coffers a command of formal English. Yet her teaching style reflects a flexibility that not only allows her students to interrogate the pedestal upon which we have placed formal English, but also to proffer alternative language styles. Let's begin with how Cathy "sounds," especially to her prospective colleagues during her telephone interview at fictitious McLeod College. The language that purportedly should get her into the "front door" is what hamstrings her in the eyes of Belle Williams who thinks her to be "white." Researchers have long grappled with what race "sounds" like. Likewise they have also studied the supposed habits that identify blacks "acting white" one of which is because they speak formal English. Cathy's own journey to standard English which included watching television newscasters and having family discussions at dinner does not hamper her from teaching her students that linguistic freedom does not necessarily mean linguistic domination and marginalization for those who do not conform to the standard. Signifyin, an often-used resistance tool in black literature, is demonstrated when Cathy reads a Br'er Rabbit[2] tale to her nephew. Henry Louis Gates (1997) calls signifyin "a form of verbal play, centering primarily on the insult, whereby people can demonstrate a mastery of improvisational rhyme and rhythm; the demonstration of such verbal mastery is a mechanism for empowerment within communities where other forms of power-political, economic-are unavailable." (310). In introducing the Br'er rabbit tales to the story, Cathy confirms the value of the stories to African heritage and culture, but also draws her mother's ire.

Cathy's tolerance for the changing reality of language allows her to analyze the profitability of rap music. Unlike, her mother Virginia, who wants words to be the same on everyone's tongue, Cathy understands and teaches that language can be reshaped—evidence of which is rap music. In her classroom, Cathy urges students to speak the language they know to articulate their understanding of pedagogy. Moreover, she convinces them that they can be part of the transfor-

---

2. Br'er Rabbit tales often pitted a weaker rabbit against a stronger fox. Ultimately the rabbit outwits the fox in every story.

mation of education that includes and encourages what Geneva Smitherman (2000) describes as a "celebration and promotion of linguistic diversity (which) must be part of the language and literacy training of youth and of their preparation for world citizenship in the 21st century (162).

* * *

Virginia Carraway

Virginia Carraway confirms Bourdieu's (1977) suggestion that the "properties which characterize linguistic excellence may be summed up in two words: distinction and correctness (60)." Virginia's version of acceptable language is modeled by white, male news anchors John Chancellor, David Brinkley, and Walter Cronkite who talked "right." By erasing their black vernacular and southern drawls, the Carraway parents "talked" their way into economic stability.

In the story, Virginia also code-switched, though unintentionally, despite her belief that language should sound the same if everyone uses it "correctly." Marty Pattillo-McCoy (1999) describes the possible reasons why Virginia code-switches, calling the practice a representation of "the linguistic negotiation of two worlds." The two worlds implied are those of the white mainstream where formal English is demanded and Pattillo-McCoy says "Black English can also be an impediment to advancement in predominately white mainstream," a point that I will explore further later in this work. White Pattillo-McCoy explores the black middle class's negotiation of the "different worlds that whites and blacks inhabit," Virginia chastises her own family members for relaxing their speech in the very manner that she herself inadvertently exercises. Using black English, as Pattillo-McCoy explains, provides a connection to the black poor (and to black culture in general for that matter) for the black middle class that distinguishes them from the white world they pilot for business/employment purposes. Yet Virginia is so absorbed with "status," that she castigates Becca and even Cathy for any slip of the tongue that leads away from English at its most polished and static form.

* * *

Becca Carraway

Becca Carraway, perhaps plays a central role in the premise of this work. That is, the formation of language on the tongue often determines the level of regard bestowed upon a person. Becca demonstrates competence in the story—a business plan that yielded a sizeable profit, being able to juggle single motherhood when her husband was on assignment and finally, saving Mr. Carraway's life after his heart attack. Yet Becca symbolizes the marginalization of not "speaking properly," in that both Cathy and her mother demonstrate a certain amount of disdain for the woman. Virginia Carraway's, contempt is more pronounced in that she not only belittles Becca and blames her for Robert Carraway's heart attack, but she also "corrects," Becca at every opportunity. Becca's purpose in the story is significant to show that language, which Virginia considers to be a powerful force, is not necessarily spoken formally by Becca, yet she succeeds in a way that Virginia does not. Granted, Becca works within a family-owned business. Yet the baseline for success (profitability, potential for growth), that is contingent upon the business plan she crafted implies that it would be just as effective if she were not in private business.

* * *

Belle Williams

Belle's character is central to the storyline and the themes inherent in this work on at least two fronts. First, Belle is the first to connect using proper English with being white, acting haughty and otherwise high-mindedness. Of Cathy, she says: "—Hell, she probably doesn't even think she's black. Sho' don't sound like it. But, Belle's prejudice for the manner in which English is spoken extends beyond "talking white." She also shows disdain for her former husband, Stephon, a Frenchman, who speaks broken English.

Belle does not necessarily code-switch, though she seems more relaxed in her conversations with her father, displaying more vernacular than she does on the campus of McLeod. What is especially interesting about this character, is how she turns the table on a recent study documented by CBS news (September 2003) which said that researchers at the University of Chicago have learned that "a black-sounding name on a resume can be an impediment," when it comes to getting responses from potential employers. The studies findings are as follows:

> White names got about one callback per 10 resumes; black names got one per 15. Carries and Kristens had call-back rates of more than 13 percent, but Aisha, Keisha and Tamika got 2.2 percent, 3.8 percent and 5.4 percent, respectively. And having a higher quality resume, featuring more skills and experience, made a white-sounding name 30 percent more likely to elicit a callback, but only 9 percent more likely for black-sounding names.

Catherine Leanna Carraway is certainly not what the author's of this study meant when they referred to "black" sounding names. And Belle, based upon her resume, and even before the telephone interview, assumes that she is white. I should admit here that this name was chosen intentionally to conceal Cathy's race until she and Belle met face-to-face.

Despite Belle's animosity toward Cathy, she unwittingly shares Cathy's belief that rap music can be a compelling and reputable means of expression. Belle says of rap: "It's really no different from da Negro spirituals dat protested slavery, or da rock music dat protested the war in Vietnam. Maybe mo' vulgar—"

Belle's exchanges with her father are crafted to reflect upon the African and African-American oral tradition. This tradition preserves a culture that Belle obviously embraces and feels a sense of obligation to preserve. While planning for her next book, Belle talks to her father about the prospect of hearing stories about McLeod College in the "old" days as reflected by Gerald. She also says she knows of other family friends who might have stories she can capture.

* * *

Gerald Williams

When Gerald Williams introduces himself to Cathy in the story, he immediately acts upon an African and African-American oral tradition of naming the young for the old and eschewing the formal use of "Jr." and "Sr." (except in the case to refer to the child exclusively as "Junior,"). For example, Gerald says: "Folk calls me old Geral'. They usted call me youn' Geral' 'cause my daddy, he was old Geral.'" Cathy comes to befriend Gerald for his stories, a validation his daughter also gives. Gerald is a key character in the story and he certainly does not use "proper" English nor judge his daughter or his new friend based upon their different ways of talking to him. Never in the story does Cathy code-switch to conform to Gerald's casual speak, and in the story they are intellectual equals based upon his expertise in the oral history of their town and her appointment as a college professor.

* * *

The extension of using Bourdieu's social background theory as the analysis for speech is to determine whether or not any language is acceptable in any venue. In the article *Talkin' Proper*, Bette Ford (1998) talks about how she was corrected in school for using the language that was socially acceptable at home, in church and in the neighborhood:

> In most of our high school classes, the teachers talked to us, and a few even invited us to talk with them. Some of them corrected the talk we brought from our homes, churches, and playgrounds—even while we were in mid-sentence they corrected us. Other teachers let us bring the language of our homes and churches and playgrounds to school.
>
> Having not come from any formal linguistic training, I borrow a phrase from the pastor of my church when I ask "Can I talk plain?"

throughout the pages of this book. This phrase is significant here for two reasons (1) I attend a black Baptist church in North Carolina. Though the congregation is comprised of many professionals in education, technology, healthcare, law and journalism, there has always been a tradition of holding a "country," "down-home" style service that attracts the masses. That means, the pastor, who is black, intersperses the occasional evidence of black vernacular in his sermons. In Spoken Soul, the authors describe black preachers like this:

> With their repertoire of styles and their passion for pageantry and dramatics, black preachers in the traditional black church don't merely deliver sermons. They hold court. When they testify for "King Jesus" in the tradition of the ancestors, the approach is eloquent, compelling. (39)

So, when the pastor asks if he can deviate from his formal text (and formal speech) to "talk plain," he recognizes and validates that the masses of black people come from a common language style that we sometimes have to revert to so that we can be sure we "understand each other." (2) Now that I have admitted to having no formal linguistic training other than the voice I can give to experience, talking plain for me means asking the audience if I can take you on an ethnographic journey. The journey is one that I believe will reveal the stories behind my passion for recognizing and wanting to appreciate the dynamism of language. Professor George Yancy, a philosopher for Duquesne University, recalls reading a paper at an academic conference only to be given a "backhanded" compliment by one of the participants, a white man. The man told Yancy: "I really enjoyed it, but why did you use *that language* [meaning African American Language]? You write very well [meaning in "Standard" American English]. You don't have to use that language to make your point." (274). Yancy continues to say that the admirer of his speech clearly believed that Yancy was being "too Black" in (his) speech, not white enough, not "proper" enough." (274). "That language" to which the white man refers when speaking to Yancy is what I mean when I join my pastor in asking "can I talk plain?"

Akin to linguist Geneva Smitherman, I attempt to "present the whole of (my) Black life" because it's from that location that I can best

"So Judas is all, show me the money, and JC is all, whatever..."

Credit: www.cardstock.com

articulate my analysis of my own language as one that exists between, what W.E.B. DuBois would call, "two warring ideals." Having a father in the military, I spent the first three years of elementary school in an American school in Stuttgart, Germany. I don't remember any thing about the teachers or the lessons, but I do recall returning to the United States, and a small town in North Carolina in particular, only to be ostracized by new black fourth grade peers for "trying to talk proud." I don't historicize the experience with dates here because the childhood experience has not compartmentalized itself into any set timetable, but has impacted virtually all of my life. Unsure of what "talking proud" meant, I consulted my sister, Shirley, who too had been accused of this transgression. We both considered that singing German songs at church and school certainly did not help our case to be accepted by our new school classmates, but we had no intention of appearing unapproachable or "proud." But, even when we cut out the impromptu Deutsch performances, the "trying to talk proud" label persisted. After my sister and I consulted with a bully, "Regina," (who incidentally befriended us after my sister made it clear we weren't afraid of her), told us that "talking proud" meant we were talking "white" and "acting like white girls." When we protested that we did not intend any differentiation, "Regina" insisted that we start acting black and that we could start with our speech: "Yall don't never say ain't or nothin' like that," she admonished. "And ya'll be trying to pick wit them looks ya'll be giving peoples." So, there it was. Even though I don't think my sister and I could articulate it at that time, we were being ostracized for speaking Standard English. Sure we had heard our share of stories from classmates using the less-than-standard version of the language (sometimes made harder to understand due to its "country" or southern tinge as well) but were nonplussed that we, who did not require a language overhaul of anyone, were being singled out for not getting it right. Nonetheless, during our weeknight dishwashing ritual we recalled the language we had heard at our respective schools, bolded and used here in sentences that mimic what we heard:

"The bus was comin' down the **skreet** and I **won't** even ready."

"Somebody stole **huh** lunch but it **won't** me."

"It's **ranging** outside."

"He always **do dat**."

"I don't even **self** know him."

"**Huh** mama came to the **do'** and he **took and** ran."

"Give me a **fowk** so I can eat my lunch."

"It costs three or **fo'** dollars."

"The older church **womens** and **mens** sit on the front row."

"That's not yours, it's **mines**."

"How many are riding **on** your car?"

"When I checked this morning **wo** 130 pounds."

"I have to say, I **looked-ed** good."

The two warring ideals part comes into play when my sister and I attempted to learn these terms in order to be accepted, then code-switched at home because our parents reprimanded us for using words that they did not consider to be words at all. But, I don't want to suggest that my family only spoke Standard English—that's simply not the case. And I never advocate that Standard English is the "right" English—or even that it is more saleable considering the profitability of rap music. Houston Baker writes about the link people must bridge between language and their personal lives versus language of oppressors. The Ebonics debate of the 1970s raised the same issue. This advice contributes to my understanding of Regina's version of English; and the assessment that Standard English is associated with the "oppressor," explains why she concluded that my sister and I were talking white or "proud." One of the best lessons I've ever learned is "you can't change where you come from." And, ultimately what might be unspoken is what we all know—"where you come from" can impact how you speak.

Chapter Two

Language in Television

What color do you hear? I sometimes ask my students this question when I ask them to close their eyes and *listen* to television. What does race "sound" like? As I was writing this manuscript, my friend David called to tell me a story about synesthesia, associating a mental image with a sound. David was watching the news and saw a Caucasian woman being interviewed by a reporter. During the interview, the woman revealed to the reporter that she was certain that an intruder in her home was a black man because he had a "black voice." The woman probably had seen enough television situational comedies to determine for herself what a "black voice" sounds like. We all do it. In creating a "common sense" experience for us through television, writers and producers use codes to help us "get" what we're supposed to get about any particular character. Language plays a key role in these conventions. Fiske (1987) speaks of this universal approach when he relays how electronic forms of popular culture shape our lives and lend meaning to them. Fiske says that society's "dominant ideological practice apparently works" because we use simplistic approaches to understanding. A predominate example of this is relating "whiteness" to "Americanness" (51). Another example of the common sense approach is seeing "realistic" or common dialogue on television that might happen anywhere. Fiske says "television tries to construct an ideal subject position which it invites us to occupy, and, if we do, rewards us with the ideological pleasure that is provided by experiencing, once again, that our dominant ideological practice, apparently, *works*: the meanings of the world and our subjectivities that is produces appear to make sense." (51).

But, language in television scripts parallel language in society in that it is synonymous with power and intelligence. The Museum of Broadcast Communications describes it as being "dichotomies" like "standard/dialect or language/vernacular" attributed in some way to an unjust allocation of linguistic power. The article on *Language and Television* continues: "In its phonetic, morphological and semantic systems language is marked by differences of class, gender, ethnicity, age, race, etc.; similarly, the speakers/hearers are also divided by their idiosyncratic knowledge of language ..." What are black characters actually *saying*? For this chapter, I look at the function of characters like "Carlton Banks" in *The Fresh Prince of Bel Air* and "Michael Evans" in *Good Times*. These characters, especially impart details about language based upon the characters they portray. I analyzed both characters within the context of their association with the primary character for each show. Finally, I reflect upon what college students believe about synesthesia—what "black" and "white" sound like on television.

Good Times (1974–1979)

Watching the Evans family on *Good Times* as a pre-teen, I could see a clear difference between the character Michael (portrayed by Ralph Carter) and his older brother J.J. (Jimmie Walker). The show, created by Norman Lear and Bud Yorkin, is set in 1970s Chicago where the Evans family faces economic marginality. The family lives in a housing project and some episodes of the show depict their experiences with unemployment, underemployment, political corruption, family loyalty, and gang violence. Two characters emerged for me as being "funny" (J.J.) and "serious" (Michael) regardless of what was going on in the Evans' household. The Museum of Broadcast Communications says the character J.J. "metamorphosed into a coon-stereotype reminiscent of early American film. His undignified antics raised the ire of the Black community. With his toothy grin, ridiculous strut and bug-eyed buffoonery, J.J. became a featured character with his trademark exclamation, "DY-NO-MITE"... Forgotten (was) Michael's scholastic success."[1] On the show, J.J.'s "costumes" include

---

1. http://www.museum.tv/archives/etv/G/htmlG/goodtimes/goodtimes.htm

footed pajamas, t-shirts with catchy phrases and a "chicken" themed work uniform. His headpieces range from a floppy jean hat to a puffy 1970s style "apple" cap. Michael, who dreams of someday becoming a lawyer and sitting on the Supreme Court, meanwhile, is typically outfitted in casual jeans and a shirt. The Museum of Broadcast Communications says of the character Michael: "(He is) thoughtful, intelligent, and fascinated with African-American history. He frequently participated in protest marches for good causes."[2] The difference in the pensive, activist character Michael, who names the streets on the standard Monopoly games after African states, and the laid back, coon antics of J.J. are captured not only in their clothing and specific roles, but also in their popularity and speech. Typically the laugh tracks occur after J.J. has spoken one of his crazy lines while the call and response pattern of "all right now," and "yeah," are reserved for the erudite talk of Michael who is frequently concerned with issues like school busing, unequal standardized tests or writing a report on a male black hero. Likewise, Michael and J.J.'s speech differ with "J.J." employing many of what Fine and Anderson cites as "ten of the most often cited syntactic features of BEV (Black English Vernacular) found in naturalistic settings."[3] They are[4]:

Feature #	Objective
1.	Deletion of the past tense marker of a verb
2.	Deletion of the -s suffix for the third person present tense
3.	Deletion of the auxiliary verb (The verbs **to have, to be, to do, will, shall, would, should, can, may, might,** and **could** are the common auxiliary verbs in English.[5])
4.	Deletion of the copula (intransitive verb that links to a subject)
5.	Use of *be* to mean habituation
6.	Negative concord (like double negatives)

---

2. Ibid
3. Fine, Marlene G. and Carolyn Anderson (1980) p. 398
4. Ibid, p. 398
5. http://englishplus.com/grammar/00000319.htm

7. Plural subject with singular form of be
8. Deletion of the -s suffix marking the possessive
9. Deletion of the -s suffix marking the plural
10. Use of a pleonastic subject

Five episodes of *Good Times* were viewed for the purposes of not only considering Fine and Andersons' hypotheses,[6] but also to look at the context in which each example of speech occurs. It appears that J.J.'s language especially reflects Fine and Andersons' hypotheses during these instances:

(1) When he is interacting with or talking about his trysts with women whom, in one episode, he calls "street foxes." He frequently uses metaphors of food to describe them. For example in one episode, J.J., an artist, swoons after a teenage girl for whom he has created a painting. Unaware that she is commissioning the painting for her boyfriend's graduation gift, the self-described "number one mama-handler in de business" writes a poem for her confessing his amour:

> How do I love thee, let me count the ways
> I love you for your skin's pure sheen
> For your two sweet lips with teeth in between
> I love you for your gorgeous bod
> And for your hair that is strictly mod
> I love you in all kinds of weather,
> 'cause baby, you **is** *alllllll* together

The underlined word "is" in the last stanza of the "poem" shows another often-used element of "black" English in that "is" is used instead of "are." And in using the metaphor of food to physically categorize his dates, he says "She's the hot sauce on my ribs. She's the bacon grease in my collard greens," using metaphor is an oratorical device utilized by African-Americans.

Even Michael confirms a variant of hypothesis number 1 in neglecting to use the past tense when revealing to his parents that he was aware of a scheme they designed to convince him to be bused to

---

6. Fine, Marlene G. and Carolyn Anderson (1980) p. 398

Cast of Good Times/Photo from The Everett Collection

a school on the white side of Chicago: "I was hip to what you <u>was</u> doing." In another episode, Michael scores low on an IQ test that he believes is culturally one-sided. As a result, he is directed to a "technical" rather than "professional" school. In this episode, black cultural idioms are highlighted to show the cultural bias of the "standardized test" and how "black" language on the test might preclude black students' unsuccessful attempts earning higher scores.

The character J.J. also confirms some of Fine and Anderson's hypotheses when (2) he describes himself: for example, he complains that he cannot be expected to be competent in high school algebra: "I ain't no Algerian." Even when a white principal speaks to the fictitious Evans family, he says "you dig" in order to relate to their vernacular. The mother of the family responds by saying "we understand." Finally, J.J. confirms Fine and Anderson's hypotheses when (3) he is speaking with his family and especially teasing his kid sister Thelma. He often uses phrases like "I gots to go" and words like dis (this) and dat (that).

Similarly, the Fresh Prince of Bel-Air employs many of Fine and Anderson's techniques especially when it comes to the primary character Will Smith.

The Fresh Prince of Bel-Air (1990–1996)

A street-wise Philadelphian comes to live with his wealthy Bel-Air relatives in this 1990s show. The freeloader, "Will" (portrayed by the rapper Will Smith) brings urban brashness to a family bent on sophistication and couth. He arrives in Bel-Air after getting in "one little fight" (according to the theme song) in his native city and sufficiently scaring his mother enough to determine that he would be better off with his California relatives. That he is fleeing urban life for a more refined and quiet life on the west coast sets the language stage for the contrast between "Will" and his cousin "Carlton" (portrayed by Alphonso Ribeiro). As with *Good Times*, I viewed five episodes of *The Fresh Prince of Bel Air* to determine the regularity with which Fine and Anderson's ten hypotheses occur. In addition, I considered other factors that resulted in the primary character ("Will") intensifying his hip-hop talk. These dynamics include: (1) When he is interacting with or talking about his trysts with women whom he calls honeys, tasties, slimmies, chubbies and squaws. The laugh track is in full effect every time Will speaks. (2) When he is speaking to his close friend "Jazz" who shares his inclination for hip-hop slang. They call each other "bruh" and greet each other with "yo" and "what up?" and use expressions like "dope" and "whack" to describe certain situations. Both characters show little respect for those in authority (in one episode, Will refers to a judge who is on the bench at his court case as "your j-ship," and (3) When he is speaking to his TV cousin Carlton (whom he accuses of acting white). Carlton a Princeton University candidate is regularly chastised by Will as being too uptight, formal and "white." In the shows, Carlton's bedtime reading is the *Wall Street Journal* and he aspires to one day become president. Like J.J. in *Good Times*, Will's costumes are attention-grabbing and colorful right down to a "souped up" version of a tuxedo and school uniform with the blazer turned inside-out, while Carlton is nattily clothed in his Bel-Air Academy issued dark coat and gray slacks. When Will attends the first day at an exclusive all-male private school, he is labeled a "resident hoodlum" who does not know the difference between former U.S. first lady Dolly Madison and the brand name for a cake company. Further, one teacher tells Will that he identifies with him because the teacher studied Langston Hughes' work while living in Harlem. In effect, the teacher typecasts Will's being black. The teacher also says of Will: "He can't be judged by our standards. He doesn't even speak our language. Where he grew up, bad means good." The teacher further engages with Will by telling him that they can listen to jazz together so that the teacher can "get down with my bad self," obviously code-switching to speak the language he expects of the "hip-hop" student. When Will requests to speak at a school board meeting to express his desire to be taught black history, the board chairman says "I'm sure it will be fly," code-switching to a language that he thinks Will will be familiar with (note: this was the first time the board chairman had seen the black student so he had no reference point for how Will would speak). This happens in another instance when Will works for a stock broker who admirably says of him "I would've lost millions (in the stock market) if not for my young homey here." Will's ne'er do well behavior in class is practically admired by not only his fellow classmates, but also the audience that laughs in the background when he says things like his response to hearing that his private school keeps memorabilia from the 1950s. Will says "man, ya'll don't throw nothin' away," (using a negative concord). Meanwhile, Carlton is portrayed as singing show tunes, conforming to rules and attempting to straighten his wayward cousin. Carlton, always quick to show the difference in his intelligence defends his cousin by saying "Excuse my cousin. He just doesn't know." Interesting too in the show, though Carlton is the incumbent classmate, the other students (all white males) pick up the new student Will's method of speech and begin using words like diss and what up. They also fashion their school uniforms after Will's, further marginalizing the "do good" Carlton whom Will describes as "Bryant Gumbel," to describe his ability to banter, especially with white people. In one episode when Carlton's father says "My son, the first black president of the United States," Carlton, incredulous asks "I'm black?" Subliminally the message is that "white" sounds like Standard English and black does not.

Contrary to Standard English's hegemony in society, in the fantasy world of *Good Times* and *The Fresh Prince of Bel-Air*, the character who speaks "hip-hop" or slang English holds the power (and gets the

Cast of the Fresh Prince of Bel-Air. Photo from the Everett Collection

laughs) as arguably both "J.J." and "Will" are the most popular characters on their respective situational comedies. It is clear that semiotics play a primary role in what language is used in television. Semiotics, the science of signs enlists a code system to present characters on television. One such code is verbal. And verbal codes appear to be abided by and thus are effective. For example, in a survey of 500 college-age students with the top answers represented here, the sound of "white" on television was considered to be:

1. Proper English, extra proper
2. Knowledgeable, educated
3. Eloquent
4. Classy
5. No slang
6. Articulate
7. Business-like
8. Arrogant

The sound of "black" on television included these answers by the same students:

1. Slang, create words
2. Jive turkey, uneducated
3. Humorous
4. Inappropriate language
5. Intoxicated

Students also shared their stories regarding the "sound" of skin color. In many instances, the reality of the world does not confirm the fantasy of shows like *Good Times* or the *Fresh Prince of Bel-Air* where the character that uses the least formal English is regarded as the most funny, the most popular or the most powerful. In fact, students' experiences illustrate that when they used Standard English they were treated in a manner quite differently from when they did not (note that all of the short statements from students have been reproduced here exactly as they were handed in with no changes to spelling or grammar):

> When I think about what black sounds like I immediately think of my sister. Even though she is clearly white I call her "ghetto." I know that I am just being superficial or stereotyping but when she uses such slang like "holler," "one,"

"pimp," and "bling." She makes me think black. She talks like some of the Rap musicians do in their songs.

* * *

I have a friend that is a manager at a local retail store. So when customers have concerns or questions they call the store and speak with him over the phone. But when they come into the store and ask for the manager; when it's him that they are already talking to, the customer looks him up and down and says "You're the one that I was talking to over the phone." He responds "yes." And it seems as though they didn't expect him to be black. Certain races must assume that black people don't use good English and that all of us talk ghetto and use broken English.

* * *

Sometime you can even speak the kings English and because of your name people assume your race. Perfect example my cousin set up and interview over the phone. During the conversation the woman was very pleasant, eager to meet my cousin. She assumed that since my cousin speaks properly and her (last) name was Brown she couldn't be black. Once my cousin arrived she saw that an African American showed up, "Mrs. Nice" disappeared and she became very cold.

* * *

Many of my family members call my parents sellouts. They say that they have forgotten their roots. My family was both raised under the poverty level. Because of their success many feel like that they have sold their self out to the white man. My mother side of the family refuses to come and visit because they say we act and live like white folks. Many of my cousins call me an Oreo because the say I look black on the outside but I white on the inside. I know we don't want to believe that there is a white and black language but there is a big difference in our culture and our language.

* * *

My husband and I like to order out from time to time. Whenever it comes time to use phone, he prefers that I be the one to place the order because he says that I sound white, therefore I get a better response.

* * *

I have learned that one can not always 'hear a voice' and determine what their race or gender is from that. An example of this, racially, could be a conversation heard on move-in day. As I was walking down the hallway of my dorm, I could hear two girls talking behind me. One was fussing about something her boyfriend has said/done to her. She was using words like: 'like', 'oh my God', 'whatever', etc. Her voice just had a white twang that could not be put into words. I assumed that she was a white girl, but when I turned around, I realized that it was a black girl.

* * *

For more than fifty years, television has been at the center of our conversations. Some of the "language" of television resembles that in our homes while often it does not.

And, true to its form, television can create a world that is inconsistent sometimes with our reality. Bette Ford says of television:

> I was a junior in high school when we got our first television. This modern miracle made a big difference in our household talk. We sat around laughing as Minnie Pearl called to us from the Grand Ol' Opry stage: "Howdee! I'm jest so proud ta be here!" In a way, she reminded me of Miss Isabel, the woman my mother used to work for. Amos and Andy were among our other early television talk models, though we didn't know any real people who sounded like either of them.

The fantasy of television is just one way that the powerless gain a voice of command. In Chapter Three, the debate goes on when the language of hip-hop music is evaluated for its ability to prove its veiled power.

Chapter Three

Language in Hip-Hop

The history of Black English has been debated for centuries. Black English discussions always occur in relation to (or even opposition to) Standard English. Standard English is that in which the "educated" are expected to use in public communication and writing, for instance. For the sake of this chapter, I will adopt Geneva Smitherman's definition of Black English as "Euro-American speech with an Afro-American meaning, nuance, tone and gesture (1977:2)." While some linguists believe that Smitherman's definition is "vague," (Daley 1998) it works nicely for this chapter which explores the relationship between English as a language of business and rap music, a genre which excels in business without the use of Standard English. "Colored English" is the term author Claude Brown uses to describe "authentic" black cultural expression that is often delivered in soul music, while author Mark Anthony Neal writes about the capacity of black popular music to fashion a "buffer" of social and use political resistance for its artists.[1] An example of this concept is the language spoken by rap music artists. Neal writes this about hip-hop/rap music:

> Hip-hop music and culture emerged as a narrative and stylistic Distillation of African-American youth sensibilities in the late 1970s ... I maintain that the emergence of hip-hop, which appeared in a rudimentary state in the mid-1970s, was representative of a concerted effort by young urban blacks to

---

1. Claude Brown refers to "colored English" in his Esquire article referenced in this work.

use mass-culture to facilitate communal discourse across a fractured and dislocated national community.[2]

Wayne Au cites these statistics about rap music in his article titled *Fresh Out of School: Rap Music's Discursive Battle with Education:*

> [H]ip-hop has gone from being a cumulative inter-American Afro-Caribbean product of Reagonomic violence on U.S. Inner cities, the booming crack trade, and massive deindustrialized campaigns ... to being a confirmed U.S. national commodity that can bring in over $1.8 billion in sales during a single year.[3]

The black church had a significant impact on the venture to unite the black community in the face of contention. Historically, through spirituals and work songs, slaves were able to "speak" to each other without white slaveholders being able to understand. Neal, like authors Michael Eric Dyson, Tricia Rose, Douglas Kellner and the like, agrees that rap music has carried on the legacy of "(giving) voice to the everyday human realities of black life."[4] Black rap artists' mastery at creating a "surreptitious" language, underscores Daley's assertion with regard to Black English semantics that it "exists in a dynamic state."[5] This dynamism is evident in the collection of slang words used by black rap artists at one moment, then discarded in favor of a "fresher" word in the next moment. Rap slang words also serve as a "secret language" that Daley says can be traced back to slavery.

Through spirituals and work songs, slaves were able to "speak" to each other without white slaveholders being able to understand. Current rap artists like Jay-Z and Kanye West rely on these same tactics to show resistance within rap language as illustrated in the following section.

---

2. Neal, What the Music Said: Black Popular Music and Black Public Culture, 136.
3. Journal of Negro Education.
4. Ibid, 138.
5. Daley, Black English and Rap Music: A Comparison.

The *Secret* Language of Jay-Z's *99 Problems* and Kanye West's *Jesus Walks*

Signifyin, an often-used resistance tool in black literature and folklore is manifested within the lyrics of Jay-Z's rap song *"99 Problems,"* and Kanye West's *"Jesus Walks."* Douglas Kellner theorizes that African-Americans use art and culture to affirm their identities and, in so doing, resist dominant ideologies. Kellner (1995) says "African-Americans have traditionally used music and musical idiom as a privileged form of resistance to oppression" (174). Black people artistically, (through film, television and music), express their political resistance more freely through their art which reaches millions of listeners. Kellner also says that black rap artists are part of a culture that use media to "resist the culture of racial oppression in the United States and to articulate their own forms of resistance and oppositional identities" (157). Signifyin is one such form of opposition, historically noted in spirituals and slave songs. Signifyin enjoys new life in Jay-Z's *"99 Problems"* and Kanye West's *"Jesus Walks."* In the *Oxford Companion to African-American Literature*, Henry Louis Gates (1997) calls signifyin "a form of verbal play, centering primarily on the insult, whereby people can demonstrate a mastery of improvisational rhyme and rhythm; the demonstration of such verbal mastery is a mechanism for empowerment within communities where other forms of power-political, economic-are unavailable" (310). Meanwhile Smitherman (1997) says signifyin' is "subtle, indirect and circumlocutory," and "it is often used to make a point, to issue a corrective, or to critique through indirection and humor (14)." The tradition of talking back to or outsmarting the master on slave plantations or planning insurrection strategies were often couched between the lyrics of gospel and slave songs. In signifyin through spirituals, the body of musical work that originated in the early 19th century when African-American slaves sought to retain traditions of African religion in the face of Christianity, slaves' secret worship meetings could incorporate African retentions in their music tradition while singing hymns from the white church. In the *Norton Anthology of African-American Literature*, spirituals are described as providing "visions of justice and peace" and "a healthful impulse to escape the sorrowful world and an implied criticism of life's earthly overwork, injustice and violence (6)." One such spiritual is *Didn't My Lord Deliver Daniel*, a reference to Daniel in the Bible being shielded from the lion's harm. The song asserts that if Daniel was delivered then certainly that day will come for all of the Lord's suffering people:

> Didn't my Lord deliver Daniel?
> An why not everyman? (Gates and McKay, 10)

Kellner says "Black literature has also been a rich source of original voices articulating the vicissitudes of the African-American experience and their culture of resistance (157). Jay-Z and Kanye West continue this tradition of "continuity and connection to Black cultural roots" (Smitherman 1997) in the present day by talking black and talking back to dominant culture through their music, even as they take pleasure in the success and power associated with that same group. Unlike historical reasons for signifyin wherein blacks had little to no recourse for true resistance, these rappers use the affirmation they receive from being popular music artists to comment on institutional racism, politics and hegemony in society. Jay-Z and Kanye West expose and resist society's conventional power structures within the lines of their rap music which is, like spirituals, "a hybrid form, combining African-American traditions with contemporary style, mixing the human voice and technology ... (Kellner 188)."

Smitherman says "rap music is rooted in the Black oral tradition of tonal semantics, narrativizing, signification/signifyin, the dozens/play in the dozens, Africanized syntax, and other communicative practices (4)." Smitherman calls the rapper a "postmodern African griot, the verbally gifted storyteller and cultural historian in traditional African society (4)."

Jay-Z has come a long way from the struggling rapper he was in 1996, trying to reach the top of the rap genre. Known for transforming rap music from what Gear magazine (2002-50) once said is viewed as "an exotic subculture," into a $1.2 billion industry.[6] Jay-

---

6. Rap CDs are a $1 billion market while DVD's are a $561 million market (Essence Magazine, August 2005).

Z, born Sean Carter in the Marcy projects of Brooklyn, New York, and also known by the monikers "Hova," "Jigga" and "Young Hov," is president and C.E.O. of Def Jam Recordings. Since his popularity soared in 1996 when his B-side song *"Ain't no n—-a,"* featuring female rap artist Foxy Brown, sold one million copies and was featured on the sound track of the 1996 film The Nutty Professor, Jay-Z has had one gold, four platinum and seven multi-platinum albums.

Jay-Z's *"99 Problems"* was featured on *The Black Album*, widely rumored to be his last in 2004. The song uses cultural context to articulate social ideologies and representations of class and race. Kellner says that critical theory "points to aspects of society and culture that should be challenged and changed and thus attempts to inform and inspire political practice" (25). Jay-Z's *"99 Problems"* relies on the strategy of signifyin to comment on the practice of racial profiling. In one stanza of his song, he raps about being stopped while driving by "the devil," a police officer. Despite feeling victimized, within the lines of the rap, Jay-Z puts himself in the same social and class category as the officer "Jake" who stops him as he talks about having enough financial wherewithal to fight the case.

In one verse of the song, Jay-Z, driving a 1994 truck that is by his definition "raw" or top of the line refers to the police officer as "Jake," a derivative of the Bible name Jacob, a "usurper" or "deceiver." Jay-Z says he pulls over rather than become involved in a highway chase because he has a "few dollars" or the means to do legal battle with the "deceptive" police officer. Over the past decade, there have been numerous reports of minority drivers' complaints that they are unfairly singled out for traffic violations. This practice, one which Henry Louis Gates (1995) termed "driving while black," has been statistically substantiated by state probes, media research, and police statistics. Jay-Z continues to describe the confrontation with the police officer, who calls him "son" hearkening back to the days of black men being called "boy," as he signifies about the reason he is stopped: because he's a black man with a hat pulled down low.

At the same time, because he feels he is being stopped gratuitously, he tells the officer he is not a mind reader and therefore does not know why he is being pulled over. Jay-Z plays on Gates' "signifyin' monkey" in making himself the protagonist whose verbal power rewards him with the capacity to expose the police officer's bias. Liberally using black vernacular English in "*99 Problems*", Jay-Z asks the officer if he's under arrest or should he continue to guess why. The officer responds by telling him that he's being pulled over for going one mile over the designated speed.

Throughout "*99 Problems*", Jay-Z code-switches from speaking in "southern" twang when he mimics the police officer's voice as he interrogates him. Then Jay-Z switches to black vernacular and slang when he's portraying and relaying what he said in the rap "confrontation" with the officer where he tells him he will not step out of his car for any reason because he is legitimately licensed to drive.

The officer retaliates at Jay-Z's knowledge of his own right to be an unharassed driver, asking if he is a lawyer or someone "important." Perhaps Jay-Z laments upon history's account of slaves and Civil Rights activists being attacked with clubs, water hoses and even dogs when the officer tells him "we'll see how smart you are when the canine's come." At the same time the officer is racially profiling the black driver to be carrying illegal drugs that will ultimately be sniffed out by dogs, the conflict also outlines the police officer's generalization of black men when he wonders if the driver (Jay-Z) is carrying a weapon. He finishes by threatening to bring a canine unit to the scene to terrorize the rapper.

"*99 Problems*" is, as Kellner describes, a "modern morality tale (162)" that illustrates how billionaire rappers like Jay-Z can fall prey to unequal and unjust distributions of power despite having the credibility to financially belong to the dominant class that reinforces class and race differences. Kellner calls rap music a genre that "articulated the experiences and conditions of black Americans living in violent ghetto conditions and became a powerful vehicle for political expression (176)." Within the lyrics of "*99 Problems*" Jay-Z confirms that he grew up in the inner city with holes in his shoes and celebrated the economic rewards of success. He also christens himself an intelligent Cinderella "rags to riches" member of the power class by acknowledging his marketing credibility and intelligence and challenging anyone who does not agree with his music to change the station.

If Jay-Z insists that he has retired from the "rap game," his protégé, Kanye West is certainly taking up his political platform. Kanye West, in his own style, signifies on what it is that a rap artist should look like. Though known more for being "preppy" than "gangsta," West's lyrics leave no misgivings about his intentions of exposing the injustices of society surreptitiously through his music. West's rap song *Jesus Walks* conforms to the body of old Negro spirituals that proffered a glimmer of hope to oppressed black people. Derrick Bell (1996) said that when slaves embraced religion often in their music, it helped them to be "free in their own minds," and "it gave their imaginations nourishment for creating a world of freedom where they could be whoever they felt they truly were" (1) In West's song, the chorus "*Jesus Walks* with me ... *Jesus Walks* ... *Jesus Walks* with them," parallels the refrains of Negro spirituals that, by signifyin, soothed blacks' hopelessness at physical abuse, subordination and inadequate living environments while offering hope in an afterlife and in knowing that a heavenly body who would ultimately purchase their liberty, walked with them.

A native of South Shore, a suburban neighborhood in Chicago, Kanye West, featured in the August 2005 issue of Time Magazine, reaped almost triple-platinum success with his 2004 debut album "The College Dropout." Owner of two multi-platinum albums of his own and more than 100 songs produced for others, he is described by Vanity Fair magazine (November 2005) as one who "awakened consciousness with his post-(Hurricane) Katrina[7] statements" wherein he criticized President George W. Bush as not caring about black people (321). Interesting enough, the clean-cut rapper who signifies on the "clean-cut" dominant culture in his rap songs is indistinguishably a member of dominant culture if judged on his own fashion style. Shunning the baggy jeans and jerseys of choice by many rap artists, West opts for business and school-boy attire reminiscent of business or "board room" fashion. Time magazine said West authored "a fresh portrait of African-American middle class angst," and that he "mixed spirituality with skepticism and rap with gospel (46)." Part of that middle class angst deals with

---

7. Hurricane Katrina caused natural devastation to the gulf coast when it struck in 2005 leaving many of the poor and black population homeless.

West's frustration at the U.S.-Iraqi war, terrorism and racism. Yet, like blacks who once relied upon Negro spirituals for comfort, he asserts that Jesus leads him the right way during moments of trials and tribulations.

West affirms Bell's point that the "survival" mechanism of black people, buoyed by religion, allows them to carve out a sense of freedom because his commentary on America's political landscape signals a determined empowerment on his part. Like Jay-Z, West also raps about unfounded confrontations with the law in *Jesus Walks*. West also uses a common ruse of rap artists, diffusing the power contained in the word "nigger," using it himself liberally throughout his rap songs, and in *Jesus Walks* referring to them as "niggaz." Further, in signifyin on the formulaic notion of "Midwestern values" of hard work, determination and fairness, West intimates that (1) those values do not advance the black population socially, politically or economically and (2) those values do not take into account that even with hard work, determination and fairness, blacks are often still on the fringe of society and (3) ultimately he has learned from his mother and his heritage that it is "Jesus" who will save black people (niggaz) from dominant culture "devils."

Kellner says "rappers also project an apocalyptic future where violence is directed against blacks. Indeed, for many rappers, the apocalypse is now" (181). Kellner also says that many of society's ills like HIV/AIDS, drug abuse and crime are believed to be a conspiracy of America's government. West says as much in *Jesus Walks*, encouraging divine intervention for those on society's fringe even as he admits that as a rapper he is not in the business of religious conversion.

By his own admission, Kanye West "can't resist a good analogy," (Vibe September 2005 page 92). *Jesus Walks* is analogous to signifyin in a traditional spiritual, *I Want Jesus to Walk with Me*, wherein desperate blacks call upon Jesus to "walk" with them during life's trials. West's version is to ask Jesus to abide with him when his feet get weary.

Virtually any resource you find mentions the fact that rap music is most often consumed by white middle-class youth. Kellner (2001) says that through rap music, black men like Jay-Z and Kanye West have carved a space for themselves to have a "powerful public voice and presence via cultural production" (376). Kanye West is featured on the cover of the February 2006 issue of *Rolling Stone Magazine* where he poses as a "Jesus" of sorts, head adorned with thorns. In the magazine, West comments about being outspoken and opinionated whether it is on national television reprimanding the president or buried within the lyrics of his rap. West says he refuses to resort to being a "house nigga," for the purpose of not offending.

Rap music presents an opportunity to make connections between signifyin of the past and its continued emergence in the present. While slave songs and spirituals of the past were steeped in fervent hope for power or even simply parity, Jay-Z and Kanye West have actually achieved it. Kevin Kearney says that Kanye West "encourages social backwardness, while showing the more privileged and educated layers that he is really an upper-middle-class, Christian yuppie who knows better." In signifyin on their rap songs Jay-Z and Kanye West not only fantasize about turning the tables of hegemony, but participate in America's power structure as well.

But even as rappers like Jay-Z and West have created a niche for themselves within the business industry, it is unlikely that their rap slang is articulated in their boardroom business. In the Village Voice, author Erik Parker reminds us that "today's rappers understand the power of their every utterance."[8] This power has resulted in rappers' endorsement of liquor, designer clothing and automobile brands showcased in their lyrics. For example, Nelly's tune about the Air Force One brand of gym shoe hearkens back to the 1980s when Run DMC hyped Adidas sneakers in their popular hit song.[9] Nelly creates a virtual commercial for the Air Force One brand by simply detailing his preference in the shoe along with his band members Kyjuan, Murphy Lee and Ali. In the song, the rappers describe the colors of Air Force One shoes they prefer, what they will do to get them, how they lace the shoes up and the difficulty or ease of procuring the shoe. The

---

8. Parker, Erik. Hip-Hop Goes Commercial: Rappers Give Madison Avenue a Run for Its Money. www.villagevoice.com

9. Nelly's "Air Force Ones" is a rap song from 2004 while Run DMC debuted "My Adidas" in 1986.

entire Nelly song is dedicated to the Air Force One brand manufactured by giant athletic wear marketer, Nike. In a USA Today news report on rap artists and marketability, the author reports that the marketability of rap artists has awakened athletic wear companies to the potential profits:

> The "casual shoes" they endorse, used more for fashion than sports, have emerged as the fastest growing piece of the $17 billion athletic footwear pie. Casual shoe sales grew 24.5% in 2004 vs. a 0.3% increase for basketball shoes and 4.6% bump for running shoes.[10]

Designer clothing and upscale watches are also rap music favorites. Rapper Li'l Kim is notorious for bragging about her preference for Gucci, Prada and Dolce and Gabbana designer labels. And rapper 50-cent has parlayed his predilection for pricey watches into a deal with the Jacob & Co. watch brand to start his own line of watches.[11] Meanwhile, Missy Elliott has been tapped to market Chrysler/Jeep's newest sport utility vehicle, the Commander. Elliott features the vehicle in her "Lose Control" video and according to Chrysler will be a useful tool in their recruitment of younger consumers. It is interesting that giant Chrysler/Jeep is enlisting a black female hip-hop artist even as its SUV products are not particularly preferred by blacks. Sarah Webster reported that "the percentage of African-American buyers of the Jeep Grand Cherokee, the largest Jeep currently on the market, is only 7.5%.[12] Missy follows rapper Snoop Dogg[13] who collaborated with former Chrysler Corporation chairman Lee Iacocca in a television commercial in 2004. Ironically, the setting for the commercial was a golf course on which, in soci-

---

10. McCarthy, Michael. *Rappers sample athletes' turf.* USA TODAY, July 4, 2005.

11. Rapper Li'l Kim's real name is Kimberly Jones while 50-cent was born Curtis Jackson. Jacob & Co. watches are the brainstorm of Russian immigrant Jacob Arabo.

12. Webster, Sarah in Rap-Up at www.rap-up.com/news/news.html.

13. Snoop Dogg is a rap artist whose real name is Calvin Broadus.

Charles V. Tines / The Detroit News—From left Lee Iacocca and Snoop Dogg.

ety, can soften the fairway for a business arrangement. Snoop, dressed in pretentious golf wear uses his trademark "izzle" words to communicate to the Chrysler boss his opinion of the automobile brand. The conversation goes like this:

> Iacocca: Nice ride
>
> Snoop Dogg: Thank you, Moca-coca.[14] Chrysler and Jeep came up on the beaucoup awards. And Dodge Trucks last as long as the D-O-Double Dizzle.[15]
>
> Plus, I've got the hookup, nephew. For sure.
>
> Iacocca: You know, I'm not too sure of what you just said.
>
> Now, everybody gets a great deal

---

14. Thank you moca-coca is Snoop's language for "Thank you much Iacocca."
15. D-O-Double Dizzle is Snoop's language for DOGG.

Snoop Dogg: For shizzle, I-ka-zizzle. If the ride is more fly, then you must buy.[16]

Iacocca: That's what I hear.

Bill Vlasic from the Detroit News called the commercial between the Chrysler pitchman and the rap artist "the most surreal pairing of spokesmen in automotive history." Vlasic writes "At age 80, Iacocca is proving once again that the art of the deal never gets old—even when he's sharing the stage with the lanky, diamond-studded, "gangsta"-rapping Snoop Dogg."

After the commercial, Iacocca told Vlasic "I don't know what the hell Snoop is saying," but he called me 'nephew,' so I guess that means I'm in." Snoop weighed in by saying to the Detroit News reporter, "It's a big company and a big-time rapper doing big business together," said Snoop. "We are bringing the generations together and it's a beautiful thing."

Snoop Dogg uses slang language to sell a conventionally middle-class white product to the hip-hop (and larger) sector. "This would have been unthinkable once," writes author Leslie Savan, "Even fifteen or twenty years ago, car makers were loath to show black people in commercials for fear that their product would be tainted as inferior, or **worse**, as 'a black car'."[17] Author Kimberly Allers writes "From Hollywood to Madison Avenue, Snoop aka Calvin Broadus, has reincarnated himself from a self-described gangster and purveyor of the pimp-and-ho lifestyle to rapper to movie star to million-dollar Main Street pitchman, appearing in ads for T-Mobile, AOL and Nokia, among others." Allers also says "Snoop, Inc. is a booming business."[18] Chrysler has further imbedded itself in the hip-hop community with its forays into Russell Simmons' May 2006 Hip-Hop Summit Action Network[19] in Miami, Florida. Chrysler representatives were on hand at the summit's "Get Your Money Right" to promote smart financial habits. Nissan, too uses rap

---

16. For shizzle I-ka-zizzle is Snoop's language for "for sure, Iacocca" while "If the ride is more fly then you must buy" is a reference to Iacocca's own marketing slogan "If you can find a better car, buy it."
17. Savan, Leslie. Slam Dunks and No Brainers. Page 48.
18. Allers, Kimberly. Essence Magazine, 2005. findarticles.com.
19. Russell Simmons is chairman of the Hip-Hop Summit Action Network.

music references in its ads. In its non-conventional ad "No Right Turns," Nissan features a group of white friends driving, but taking no right turns. The journey takes them to places they would not otherwise have thought of going. At the end of the commercial, they all sing a phrase from rapper Jay-Z's song "Can I get a What What."

Avis Rental Car's hilarious ads featuring three white straight-laced business men in suits, is set to rap music by the artist Lumbajac. The men are mouthing the words to the song "2 g's" which is all about getting their hands on money. Yet, when a mobile phone rings in the car, they turn down the music and take a call, presumably from their boss or a client they are traveling to see. When they turn down the music one of the men says "Hello Sir. 20 minutes away. Yes, sir." After clicking off the call, the three men resume playing the loud rap, posturing as they lip-sync the song. While rap music is wholly acceptable for the trio while riding in the car, the music form is seemingly not appropriate for the negotiations necessary to yield the "cheese" Lumbajac raps about. Unlike Snoop Dogg as he chats with a former Chrysler chief, the men quickly resort to speaking Standard English with the person on the other end of the telephone. And, over at Nextel, a rap song "Push It" by Salt n Pepa is used to promote the popular mobile telephone.[20] In a scenario similar to that of Avis' commercial, three white men are dancing to the rap hit when a colleague rushes in panicking about the whereabouts of a product for a customer. The men stop the music, check on the status of the product then return to listening to the song. And Hewlett Packard joins the list of advertisers enlisting the services of rap artists to endorse their products. Though his face is hidden, the rapper Jay-Z[21] provides voiceover for Hewlett-Packard's personal notebook computers. His face is obscured but the lower half of his body is shown decked out in a designer suit and at the conclusion of the commercial, he gives the familiar hand signal for Rocafella enterprises as he speaks:

> "I gotta track all my investments because I'm retired, *right*? My passport says Shawn, but you may know me by another name. Holla."

---

20. Salt and Pepa are female rap artists who sang "Push it" in the late 1980s.
21. Jay-Z's real name is Shawn Carter.

Mark Lelinwalla from Vibe.com says:

> "HP had Jay introspectively speaking about his various endeavors and individual traits to drive home its campaign slogan—'The computer is personal again.'"

Meanwhile, Mimi Valde's says:

> HIP-HOP IS big business. In fact, in CD sales alone, it's a $1.2-billion industry. In addition to records, it drives sales in fashion, film, books and energy drinks. No other entertainment genre inspires this sort of consumption.

and

> There's something really beautiful about all the different ways to experience hip-hop. Besides the opportunities for jobs beyond artist or producer, it's nice to see something that started in the 'hood has become a valuable tool that even corporate America uses to sell its products. Nike, McDonald's and Hewlett-Packard have all tried to incorporate hip-hop into their marketing. These and other companies have apparently gotten over their inability to understand the lyrics and instead focused on the most important fact about the music: Hip-hop is all about aspiration.[22]

In *Spoken Soul*, the authors astutely remind us that:

> Some Americans embrace spoken soul (albeit subconsciously) only when it's delivered over the FM dial, crooned in a ballad, or draped atop the thud-thud of a funky baseline. Not that vernacular pronunciation and syntax are obscured when set to music, for they often take on an even grander flavor—becoming even more evocative and "in your face" when jazzed up for twelve bars or worked over a catchy

---

22. Vales, Mimi from 'Hood goes Corporate, November 2005, Los Angeles Times. http://www.latimes.com/news/printedition/suncommentary/la-op-hiphopcommercial27nov27,1,133690.story?coll=la-headlines-suncomment.

hook. It is then that Spoken Soul's aptness for expressing the exotic in the plainest of terms, for expressing the unremarkable with the greatest flamboyance, and occasionally, for expressing concepts that Standard English simply cannot becomes obvious."[23]

Clearly rap artists and rap music are considered marketable commodities for even the most traditional companies. And, while the lyrics of their rap songs audaciously pervade commercial frames, sometimes a message other than "acceptance" is being advanced. The actors in both the Avis and the Nextel commercials suggest that the rap music they are listening to certainly has no position in the business world they navigate. Yet the consumers who view the commercial are keenly aware that rap music is part of the sales pitch. Savan says "white attempts to yo[24] here and dis[25] there are an important piece of identity-and-image building for individuals and corporations alike."[26] Savan continues by saying "Black talk has openly joined the sales force."[27] But, I detect that the black pop music craze in no way threatens the "expected" language of business. Rap artists create and tweak words like fresh, dope, def, 24s.[28] And, the youthful rapper Bow Wow even has a song, Fresh Azimiz (Fresh as I'm is) chock-full of words you likely wouldn't hear in anyone's board room: homie, thuggin', whippin'.

Allers says that the intersection of rap artists and advertising is a result of "corporate America's quest for the hottest and hardest-to-reach consumer demographics—men and teens."[29] And, when Allers asked one company vice-president why he selected a rapper to hawk his product, the reply was along the lines of attracting a youth audience and associating "fun" with the company's product. Placing a product in their videos can net a rap artist anywhere between $10,000

---

23. Spoken Soul page 73.
24. Yo is slang for "hey."
25. Dis is slang for "disrespect."
26. Savan, Leslie. Slam Dunks and No Brainers. Page 48.
27. Ibid.
28. Words heard in some rap songs.
29. Allers, Essence Magazine. www.findarticles.com.

and $35,000.[30] Says Au "Rappers and rap music are used by major corporations to sell almost anything: movies, soft drinks, clothing lines, pizza, deodorant, candy, Internet services, shoes, beer, cars, potato chips and sporting events (from Morrell& Duncan-Andrade, 2002)."[31]

But even as rap artists promote items from A to Z, and perhaps the art of hip-hop is being co-opted by the business of hip-hop, they certainly can't use their pop language to transact business and be taken with any degree of seriousness. While dress code is certainly not the premise of this work, when NBA Commissioner David Stern instituted a dress code for the predominately black basketball league, the writing on the wall was that business practice would prevail even in the sports arena.

In a 2003 BBC report, the Campaign for Real Education implored teachers to help improve students' language in order to make them more favorable candidates for the workforce.

According to the report, "street slang made popular by rap music artists and wider TV cultures, is making thousands of youngsters unemployable."

Author John Clancy's work on business language metaphors in *The Invisible Powers: The Language of Business,* considers that business organizations utilize metaphors like "the man at the helm, who has the ball, what's the game plan," (11). And, as Clancy's intriguing work eloquently explores how an "institution builder (may) convince a wealth seeker, or vice-versa, about the nature and purpose of a business," shifting paradigms and business methods (174), it does not consider what type of language will be utilized to transact that business or whether or not that language will include "rap" slang.

Renee Blank and Sandra Slipp interviewed black employees in corporate America and say "many African-Americans say that the need to conform to white norms of management style saps them of their identity. (24)." One black receptionist even said:

---

30. Ibid.
31. Au, Wayne, "Fresh out of School: Rap Music's Discursive Battle with Education. Journal of Negro Education.

"Hi Honey, I'm homeboy."

Credit: www.cardstock.com

"I always think about my speech—whether it sounds 'white' enough" (24). Still another black employee admits "many whites don't understand that most blacks are bi-cultural—they grow up learning how to act in both the white world and the black world" (25). And still another employee interviewed said that white co-workers said she did not behave "black." The worker said: "When I ask what does acting black mean, the answer always reflects the ghetto images in the media or criminals, sports figures, musicians, rappers."

In his book titled *The Sociology of African American language*, Charles DeBose, a university professor says that degrading "black" language is just one of many ways in which black people have been typically stereotyped and stigmatized for centuries. There are certainly some asides when it comes to portraying "black" sounding things as negative. Crooner Joss Stone, who also questions how "black sounds" is often described as being a "soulful" singer. According to music.yahoo.com, when it comes to music "people hear more than just sounds. Usually, the more "soulful" one sounds, the "blacker" they are assumed to be." Stone, herself is puzzled by this revelation, saying "Music has no color. How can it have a color because you can't see it? How can you say that I sound black or white, or purple or pink or whatever?"

As I am discussing the topic of this manuscript with my next door neighbor Terry Paige, he lights up with information to tell. It seems that in his first job as a securities analyst on Wall Street, he, a Florida transplant to New York Terry learned that there would be something unconventional for him in his job orientation schedule. While he expected lessons on the culture of the company, rules and regulations, he did not quite anticipate an orientation in how to speak on the job. Terry said he appreciated the training because he did not want to be discriminated against by securities customers alerted to either his "southern" accent or his "black" accent who might be turned off by either or both. Other companies offer continuing education courses with topics from Cross-Cultural Business Communication and Understanding Cultural Differences to workplace culture and verbal communication.

Even as institutions like banks consider innovative and efficient ways to communicate with customers, the manner in which that communication will take place is being pondered. The goal so far is to ensure that new means of communications like (Internet) "chatting," and instant messages which often utilize slang and abbreviated words conform to standardized business rules. According to an article posted in the Banking Strategies publication, Wells Fargo is one company that wants to keep pace with novel communication modes

"Yo! Check it out!"

Credit: www.cardstock.com

but insists that its representatives continue to adhere to business standard so much so that the company checks instant message transcripts from their representatives to promote compliance. The article does state however, that some businesses recommend a more laid-back form of instant written communication even allowing for representatives to delve into the personal lives of their customers via email and instant messaging.

A former university instructor, Paul Franklin Ryder weighs in to say that the use of slang in no way can harm the hold formal language has on business practice: "People will continue to self-censor when writing formal documents like job applications or university essays where it is in their own interest to conform to common practice."[32]

---

32. http://www.rediff.com///netguide/2003/may/07slang.html.

The message is certainly a mixed one when corporations like McDonald's strive to be a "friend" to its younger employee set by designing "cool" uniforms, enlisting "cool" celebrities and athletes to advertise their burgers and using a slogan like "I'm lovin' it." But, the ultimate understood message might be to fill in your job application using Standard English if you seriously want to get hired.

Chapter Four

Language in Society

Nestled in picturesque York, South Carolina, sits York Comprehensive High School. Located in the county seat, York Comprehensive High School is home to about 1100 students. Curious to learn student opinions on the intersection of "rap" oriented language with formal situations, I surveyed approximately 50 students in an English composition course to determine what version of the English language they considered appropriate in specific situations. The students ranged in age from 15–16. I combined the answers given by the high school students with those answered by 50 random college students in the student center at the University of North Carolina at Charlotte, the fourth largest institution in the 16-campus state system. The college students ranged in age from 17–31. Finally, I collected surveys from 50 random people at a local shopping center in the eastern portion of the city of Charlotte where one retailer in the local city newspaper is quoted as saying "you've got to understand the power of urban hip-hop. We've got (a) market that no one else may be tapping into. We have to have a niche."[1] The participants at the shopping center ranged in age from 18–57. The racial composition of all three sets of students varied and no data was collected on their personal backgrounds. Although question seven asked the respondents' ages, this information was not used in any significant manner in assessing and evaluating the results.

---

1. The Charlotte Observer, June 10, 2006. Page 2D.

In delivering the survey,[2] I began with a list of slang words collected from popular television shows, rap songs and students in my classes. Paris Hilton's[3] frequent axiom *"That's Hot"* on FOX television's *The Simple Life* television show (2003) certainly made the list along with Snoop Dogg's "fo shizzle my nizzle." The survey (Appendix A) and the larger results are as follows:

Appendix A
Survey

Please look over the words listed below. Then, read the seven questions below and circle the answer that applies to you. There is no right or wrong answer.

1. You know what I'm sayin'
2. That's what's up
3. Holla back
4. How bout'cha
5. Holla at ya boy/girl
6. What's up
7. Mos def
8. Whatev
9. I'm mad 'bout that
10. What it is
11. That's hot
12. For real though
13. Fo shizzle my nizzle

(Continued on next page)

---

2. Refer to Appendix A for survey questionnaire.
3. Paris Hilton is a Hilton Hotel heiress who is well known for saying "that's hot" on the television show 'The Simple Life.'

1. Do you use any of these words on a daily basis?		YES	NO
2. Do you use these words with friends?		YES	NO
3. Do you use these words in a "business" or "formal" situation. (Example: on a job interview, talking to teachers?)		YES	NO
4. Do you feel the need to use "proper" English when you are transacting business, at work or at school?		YES	NO
5. Do you feel comfortable speaking as you do in any situation?		YES	NO
6. With rap music being a billion dollar business, do you think that the language of rap is acceptable in any setting?		YES	NO

7. What is your age? _____

The slang phrases used for the survey were compiled by eight students between the ages of 20–21 at the University of North Carolina at Charlotte. The students are quoted as "respondents" in later references in this chapter, providing narrative regarding the survey questions in this text. Demographically, four of the students identified themselves as African-American while the other four students identified themselves as Caucasian. The students worked together to compile the list of phrases. Upon completion, I tested the language used in the survey to determine its ease of understanding. For question number two, I asked the eight students how they defined "friends." In general the answers were: acquaintances, someone (I) do social things with, someone I feel comfortable with and someone (I) let my guard down with.

The eight students stated that they needed no clarity with regard to what a "business" or "formal" setting was. In fact, examples are given right on the survey (on a job interview, talking to teachers).

When I asked the eight students to give me their definition of "proper" English, the answers I received were Standard English and English with no slang. They indicated that they needed no clarity for understanding question number five. When I asked the students to define "the language of rap" for me the answers were: the slang words

Credit: www.cardstock.com

and phrases in question number one, words that rappers use in their songs and "street" language.

Question 1

Do you use any of these (slang) words on a daily basis?

	YES	NO
York Comprehensive High School Students	48	2
University of North Carolina at Charlotte	36	14
Shopping Center in Charlotte, North Carolina	45	5

According to NTC's Dictionary of American Slang, "there is no standard test that will decide what is slang or colloquial and what is not." The dictionary goes on to say that "slang is rarely the first choice of careful writers or speakers or anyone attempting to use language for formal, persuasive or business purposes." And, in his article in *American Speech*[4] Moore talks about the progression of slang into mainstream widespread practice:

> The process begins with a term becoming widely used to refer to a set of values that have special appeal for a generation of adolescents and young adults ... The set of values serves as the core referent of the slang term, and the enduring quality of these values underlies the longevity of the basic slang term for a given generation. As this cohort matures the basic term continues to be a prominent part of its vocabulary and is likewise taken up by those cohorts that follow immediately in its tracks. The new term will endure as a basic slang expression until another dramatic shift in generational values calls forth a new term with which the new rebellious younger generation identifies itself and distinguishes itself from its elders.[5]

Of the 150 people sampled, an average of 43 people said they use slang words listed on the survey on a daily basis compared to an average of 6 people who do not use the

Question 6

With rap music being a billion dollar business, do you think that the language of rap is acceptable in any setting?

	YES	NO
York Comprehensive High School Students	47	3
University of North Carolina at Charlotte	45	5
Shopping Center in Charlotte, North Carolina	45	5

---

4. Moore, Robert L "We're Cool, Mom and Dad are Swell: Basic Slang and Generational Shifts in Values. *American Speech*, 2004

5. Ibid. Page 63

It was in 2001 that renowned scholar Cornel West released *Sketches of My Culture*, his compilation of rap songs about black culture. An audience gathered at prestigious Harvard University to hear songs from West's debut foray into rap music.[6] Fellow scholar Michael Eric Dyson, who is also a minister, calls himself "an intellectual deejay or emcee trying to negotiate a range of dialogues and discourses," and says "humans are always switching among different vocabularies and voices while trying to understand ourselves and our culture."[7] That two preeminent scholars embrace hip-hop as a means of expression is critical to considering the possibilities for the language of rap outside its traditional venue. In *Speaking in Tongues* authored by Angela Spivey, Dyson advises:

> Language is crucial to understanding the questions of identity that blacks and all Americans wrestle with, (Dyson says) because language reminds us that we exist at all. The complex identities of blacks are expressed in forms as wide-ranging as the preaching of Martin Luther King, Jr., the gangsta' rap of Snoop Doggy Dogg, and the writing of James Baldwin. Using many languages, speaking in many tongues, is a habit of survival that African-American people across the board have learned (he says). For instance, young blacks must learn the rules of common English usage, of street speech, and of the dialects and social accents of their own region or turf.[8]

Considering West and Dyson's endorsement of language forms remote from those used in the traditional "specialized academic language,"[9] question six on the survey I gave considered whether respondents believed that the language of rap is acceptable in any setting. This question specifically addressed not so much whether or

---

6. Cornish, Audie N. Harvard Professor Makes Hip-Hop CD. The Washington Post.com. Tuesday, Nov. 6, 2001.
7. Spivey, Angela. Speaking in Tongues obtained from website: http://research.unc.edu/endeavors/end1295/tongues.htm.
8. Ibid.
9. Ibid.

not the respondents felt comfortable using hip-hop language in any setting, but rather if they believed it would be received favorably outside the creative musical world. Dyson, who is described by Spivey as being efficient in merging the languages of "the church, the academy, and popular culture"[10] says "People have attacked scholars, (he says) as speaking in jargon-bloated discourse that has no relevance to people."[11] The survey results for this question are relevant with regard to Dyson's quote. Ninety one percent (91%) of the respondents in this survey said that they did indeed think the language of hip-hop was acceptable in any setting while only 9% agreed that it was not acceptable in any setting. These results strongly conflict with the answers in question four when 28 of the 150 respondents, or 85% of those surveyed said that formal English should be spoken when transacting business, when at work or at school. Why such disproportion? While the raw data collected does not reveal the answer to this question, the narratives in Chapter Five suggest that individuals are taught "appropriate" language uses in some version of formal education and have retained this information, a point that is emphasized by author Bette Ford who recalls the period in her life when she started watching television, and later how the language of schooling impacted her fixation on slang:

> It must have been during this same period of my youth that my fascination with slang began. Across the years, the same meanings have acquired different slang expressions: *I can dig it, I'm hipped; I know what's happening, I know what time it is; groovy, right on, cool; coolin' it; cool out, chill out.* I still like slang. But someone told me it's not always proper.
>
> I think I've always written in the "proper" language. In high school, I did a little writing. I also remember conjugating verbs and diagramming sentences. Our tenth grade teacher devoted the whole year to diagramming. I still remember the

---

10. Ibid.
11. Ibid.

book. It was called *Sentence Structure Visualized.* I was pretty good at diagramming. I made A's in the class.

Chapter Five

Language Possibilities in the Classroom

For me, everything returns to my being a teacher and using popular culture, opposition to the dominant and terrain of struggle to teach alternate possibilities. Does rap music's financial validation make it a useful linguistic option for the classroom? Students enter my classroom nowadays and I have noticed that they do not see a need to code-switch for the erudite "teacher." They email me from their wireless devices in an unthinkable grammar for a college student. But I think it is just fine. Language—even hip-hop certainly has possibility for pedagogy. The classroom instructor has a forum in which to change perceptions of language. Angela McRobbie says that "if representation remains a site of power and regulation, as well as a source of identity, then cultural academics working in the fields of representation have a critical job to do in attempting to recast these terms by inflecting new meanings." In this chapter, I inquire about alternative ways of learning. Can an academic setting also be a space to explore the language of rap music/hip-hop, slang, etc.? As I deliberated about what such a curriculum would look like and why it would be useful in the likely event I had to defend it, I recalled one of my own youthful experiences which particularly applies here. In seventh grade, I wrote a poem that was published in a booklet called "Patchwork," named so because my teachers who produced the booklet said it was a compilation of bits and pieces of everyone's writing much like a patchwork quilt. Prior to seeing the final result, I envisioned a booklet with a stream of thought from one seventh grader merging with a stream of thought from another. I remember my restlessness the night before the booklet was to arrive, fresh from the press, to our school. I wondered how anyone would recognize my poem if the words were mixed in with everyone else's. How would they know what I was really trying to say? To my delight, when I saw the final version of Patchwork, only the cover showed any resemblance to a "patchwork quilt." Inside, each student's literary work was represented in its entirety, and most importantly in its own space. I was relieved that the poem I wrote stood alone on a page with my name listed as the author and that whoever picked up a copy of Patchwork would be able to follow exactly what I was saying in my poem. They would get a sense of who I was by what I wrote.

As I look back on how significant it was for me to be recognized by my words, I therefore recognize the value of my students' "stories" and the relevance of their personal experiences. I feel compelled to help liberate and empower them in the college classroom by giving them an opportunity to share those experiences. Representation and identity has been a patchwork of sorts created by the onslaught of electronic media images. Many of my students protest the way they are portrayed by media. My minority students especially have lamented that they believe that their portrayal by media precludes the talents they bring with them into a college classroom and that they are frequently "misunderstood" based upon their misrepresentations. Language typically has played a key role in their stories. I considered how I could use my own experiences of searching for my voice and my own identity, to coming full-circle as a scholar, to place more emphasis on students defining themselves even as they struggle with how they are defined linguistically by popular culture. How can I give my students the type of relief I felt when I opened Patchwork and found my poem, a true representation of me, on a page by itself? To engage with McRobbie, I turn to bell hooks who says that theory is created by those in pain. The black males in my courses tell me that they recognize that they are lambasted by media images that portray them as thugs and slicksters who speak an objectionable slang. Yet, if we let go of our tightly held traditional social practices, we can envision things quite differently and disarm the potential for language to become the advocate for emphasizing what Delpit and Dowdy call the "false assumptions about intelligence, family background, morality or potential." To start this process, I examine my sense of guidance in the classroom. hooks (1994) says that "to teach in a manner that respects and cares for the souls of our students is essential if we are to provide the necessary conditions where learning can most deeply and intimately begin." The experiences students bring with them into the classroom are just as valuable as any knowledge I gained in a graduate school textbook. Through my work in turning minority representation and culture into the topic of my intellectual practice, I am able to illuminate those stories that students carry like luggage with them into the classroom some of which follow:

> I work for a museum and I encounter the verbal language code misunderstanding often. My name is common among races and cultures. When I am on the phone with donors or other museum professionals, I try to sound "professional" regardless of my race. Sometimes, when people meet me, see that I am African-American, the facial expressions are priceless. However, I overlook them and still carry on with utmost professionalism until what was obvious is no longer a factor.

* * *

> The language of rap is created in a specific environment, it helps those in that environment explain and relate to one another. Unfortunately, even though rap is a billion dollar business, those who run this business are not those who come up with the language. We do have a few rapper that have made themselves into power players in the rap industry it's still not enough to change the world.

* * *

> In today's society, one who does not carry themselves in a more positive manner that does not include rap language on a regular basis could be looked down upon.

* * *

> I do not think that "language of rap" (slang, hip-hop words, etc.) is inappropriate in every situation. I believe that this type of language has been associated negatively by the ma-

jority of people and therefore it is going against the "norm" or accepted behavior in certain settings, like job interviews, work, and classrooms. However, this is only an association that has developed. Some people relate rap to rebellious youth and criminals. But I believe that it is just another form of expression and just another type of language that is very widely used but not widely accepted.

* * *

Although you may not notice, your coworkers and employers pay attention to the way that you carry yourself. Even though slang seems like something that is very minor it may keep you from advancing in your place of work

* * *

In my personal opinion I don't think we should conform our verbal code. I think our language is part of who we are and the atmosphere we grew up in. If you are articulate and well spoken be true to that or if you come from a culture where slang is how you express yourself be true to that. If we attempt to change our verbal language it appears fake and rehearsed but, when we stay true to it you are better understood by society and authentic.

* * *

In certain classroom settings I believe a certain degree of hip-hop jargon is necessary to create an environment conducive to growth and maturation of today's high school students. This makes class enjoyable, which supports the age old theory that if you love what you're doing, you will excel at it.

* * *

I'm scared to even make a typo at work because being black, it would categorize me as being dumb when it was simply a mistake. When it comes to anything to do with English I

worry about how I sound or write. When I get home is when
I can relax and talk the way I talk.

Perhaps the most commanding quote from students was this one: "In a perfect world people should be able to speak the way they feel most comfortable. Unfortunately, that is not the case." hooks (1994) says "we can teach in ways that transform consciousness, creating a climate of free expression that is the essence of a truly liberator liberal arts education." With that quote I begin to not only illuminate my students' stories but also explore the possibilities for language that can validate every individual.

Freire (1970) endorses "co-intentional education" where a student and teacher create reality and knowledge as a team and "through common reflection and action, they discover themselves." By collecting students' stories I began this process. A classroom conducive to an optimum learning experience for all students is another step in equipping students to deal with pop culture's archetypal categorizations for language. A culturally inclusive curriculum helps to facilitate this process, especially since language plays a major role in culture. It is essential that students see a pertinent connection between our class discussion and their lives outside of class.

Maxine Greene (1978) says that too many individuals in our society experience a feeling of domination and powerlessness. Such is certainly the case when my students feel helpless to media portrayals and representations and suffer embarrassment when others confuse their language, personalities and beings as one of a media-produced character. Taking a critical look at perceived power is certainly part of the education process in the classroom. In fact, Giroux and Simon (1989) say that questioning power is a key part of the teaching and learning process. Therefore, as a teacher, I strive to motivate students to become more critical of what they see and, as Greene calls it, to be "wide awake" as they think about the things that dominate them. In my class the complaint is often language representation. A wide-awake student is receptive to alternatives and active in making change. A wide awake student is also in full grasp of a sense of his own reality and life at every moment. And, wide awake students are critically aware of their capacities and do not allow themselves to be suppressed. A wide awake student is self aware and has a "clarified sense" of his/her own reality. hooks (1994) says that teachers are the catalyst for creating change in the classroom as they work to engage all students to invite them to be active participants in learning. Ensuring that students realize they can make a contribution in my classroom is always a goal, as those moments of cross-cultural and respectful dialogue contribute not only to their learning experience, but mine also. I recognize that their knowledge is not only a reflection of their dialogue with me, but also with their fellow students.

In reflecting about what experiences students bring into the classroom with them on a daily basis, I recognize that there is more to them than what I see. While I may see a 20-something student sitting before me waiting to embark on a learning experience about how popular culture representations impact their lives, there is often so much more. Students' backgrounds are so multi-faceted and their own location of their feelings can often reflect those varied backgrounds, making for quite a dynamic in the classroom.

Gloria Ladson-Billings explores the dynamic triangulation between student–teacher and schooling. A proponent of teaching toward personal empowerment and liberation, Ladson-Billings encourages mixing scholarship and story. Like, Ladson-Billings, I utilize the "culturally relevant" mode of teaching to prepare and question students as they confront injustices in their life. To that end, I see my job as collaborative with the students, where heuristic learning takes place. "Good teaching involves enriching, not impoverishing, students' understandings of self, others, and the world," according to David Hansen. He calls teaching a "moral and intellectual practice with a rich tradition." The blueprint to effective teaching of multicultural students impacted by media, or any students for that matter, first involves cultivating the student. Coach them to talk and to feel comfortable hearing their own voices. Next, teach indirectly. That is, use the information from other students in order to make key points about social situations. Finally, Hansen says that teachers should "address the place of both tradition and ideals in teaching." In returning to Hansen's claim that teaching is a moral and intellectual practice rooted in tradition, I can foresee breaking tradition to consider some language alternatives that Delpit and Dowdy call "positive ways to view the different languages that students bring to school, thus affirming and including all students."

Teaching Slang, Hip-Hop and Idioms in the Classroom

Dan Byrne asserts that "slang terms are important to an ever-changing society, especially for minority ethnic groups." At the same time they are virtually valueless in the classroom. But, in order for students from all walks of life to be comfortable with their personal story, we might consider validating the language in which it is relayed. There are other reasons too. For example, David Burke recalls his experiences with a student who was not a native speaker of English. Considering the slang that we inadvertently and even intentionally use in our day to day conversations, he determined that nonnative English speakers would need quite a bit of coaching to be able to understand the language completely "because our language is loaded with nonstandard English, i.e. slang and idioms." Burke says that to not teach slang in the classroom is to undermine and eliminate a whole other part of speaking English. Burke says, "imagine someone not familiar with idioms being told during a meeting that he or she 'has the floor' or being asked to 'take the ball and run with it.'" Burke says, and I am of the same opinion that the goal is not to necessarily encourage slang use but to acquaint others to this form of language. As educators working with a multicultural audience, the aim is to diminish the incidences where students feel like "others" or outsiders or that their means of communication are of no value. In Melvyn Bragg's book The Adventure of English: The Biography of a Language, he says "English is open to every influence, however insignificant the source might be." To give voice to other possibilities for language supports the global perspective most educational institutions strive for. Geneva Smitherman says we can "focus on language as a dynamic communication system used in everyday discourse, rather than as a frozen set of rules confined to the pages of a grammar text." Thus we recognize and provide a platform for the reality that students' socialization and life experience comes from the conversations they have had with their families, in their churches and with their peers. All of these occasions complement the theories that might be addressed in a popular culture course for instance and play a key role in the learning practice. In recalling her own teenage years, author Bette Ford says:

> I have continued going from my home, church, and playground to school, and the words from all these places still speak to me. They always will, for they all hold *proper* places in my head and in my heart. Through all these words, I have been taught.

In our traditional efforts to maintain the distinct qualities of English that include buzz words like correct pronunciation and grammar, in Language and Symbolic Power, Bourdieu reminds us that:

> The fact remains that social science has to take account of the autonomy of language, its specific logic, and its particular rules of operation. In particular, one cannot understand the symbolic effects of language without making allowance for the fact, frequently attested, that language is the exemplary formal mechanism whose generative capacities are without limits.

Bourdieu, like Smitherman considers that language is not static but instead is constantly recreating itself in different, exciting and even suitable forms. Hip-hop language is one such form of language whose exploration in the classroom produces fascinating stories and insights into popular culture. Hip-hop frequently serves to offer insight into culture and socialization of a population. Students who identify not only with the language of hip-hop, but also the stories contained within the genre bring a fresh perspective obviously to popular culture courses, but also to subjects like folklore, political poetry and history courses. In a Los Angeles Times news article, Lin, Rong-Gong, II comments on the value of hip-hop in the classroom:

> Can one really compare the works of Robert Frost, one of America's most lyrical poets, with the edgy words of rapper

Eminem? Apparently, yes. That was one of the messages delivered Saturday at a conference of 400 educators and students at a South Los Angeles middle school. The goal was to promote rap as a way to reach children in the classroom. "You're always hearing about the disengagement of urban youth" from schools, said Patrick Camangian, an English teacher at Crenshaw High School. Rap can be a bridge, he said." Why not use that culture to connect?" added Mark Gonzales, a UCLA graduate education student and an organizer. "It allows them to engage."

Teachers who reported on their integration of hip-hop and its language in their curriculum admitted advantages that included socializing non-native speakers to the language, increased student interest and participation and a connection between students' lives and their school work. Bourdieu says "the competence adequate to produce sentences that are likely to be understood may be quite inadequate to produce sentences that are likely to be *listened to*." Yet, when students can see compatibility between their experience and their education, the communication gap is narrowed. Bourdieu continues by saying that "social acceptability is not reducible to mere grammaticality. Speakers lacking the legitimate competence are *de facto* excluded from the social domains in which this competence is required, or are condemned to silence." Clearly as popular culture seeks the means to struggle against the power of dominance, they look for alternate ways to succeed. Hip-hop music and language has been one technique to give voice to the voiceless.

The Education Alliance at Brown University developed *The Diversity Kit: An Introductory Resource for Social Change in Education* that speaks to the uses of diverse forms of language in the classroom and "brings together current research on human development and cultural diversity." The kit also "explores issues of diversity in education that are essential for schools and teachers who are committed to quality education for all students." The project advocates for school linguistic flexibility and promotes the objective that "no single style of communication should be deemed the only acceptable one in the classroom" which is not to say that Standard English will not be the objectives. Instead, the goal is to promote significance of the language form that students arrive to class with and complement it with formal varieties considering that "so called 'Standard English' is simply one form among many equally valid and complex varieties of English" (Crystal 1987 quoted in the Diversity Kit). The Diversity kit gives an outline of what an ideal complementary language curriculum might entail (Appendix C) using black English as the model. The instructional strategies are not exhaustive, but they serve to initiate discussion of possible additional teaching strategies.

Appendix C

Adapted from the Diversity Kit
Education Alliance
Brown University

Dialect Conflict	Instructional Strategy
Omitting final consonants (col' instead of cold)	Merely point out the difference between the student's pronunciation and the Standard English pronunciation
Use of "to be" verb patterns (You be playing all the time)	Practice alternate ways of articulating action words
Omission of the copula (to be) or the possessive (She glad about her sister birthday presents)	Merely point out the difference between the student's pronunciation and the Standard English pronunciation
Students use their "home" or "comfort zone" cultural language patterns in all situations	Suggest that there is a time and a place for patterns of English. Help the student determine when and where to apply different English forms.
Students write in the same way that they talk	Direct the student in determining when oral patterns (like repeating words) are useful in giving a written document "effect" as opposed to being superfluous.

In *Doing Cultural Studies: Youth and the Challenge of Pedagogy* by Henry Giroux, the author convinces us that educators might address the changing demographics of youth by seeking another perspective on what he calls the "relationship between culture and power, knowledge and authority, learning and experience, and the role of teachers as public intellectuals." Cultural Studies is one such subject area that acknowledges a diverse student body that is influenced by media, shifting economics, politics, family background and the like. Giroux adds that "traditionally, this has been a culture of exclusion, one which has ignored the multiple narratives, histories, and voices of culturally and politically subordinated groups." A non-traditional language practice in the classroom is one means of modification. Giroux states that "at stake here is the attempt to produce new theoretical models and methodologies for addressing the production, structure and exchange of knowledge" and:

> as youth are constituted within languages and new cultural forms that intersect differently across and within issues of race, class, gender, and sexual differences, the conditions through which youth attempt to narrate themselves must be understood in terms of both the context of their struggles and through a shared language of agency that points to a project of hope and possibility. It is precisely this language of difference, specificity, and possibility that is lacking from most attempts at educational reform.

When I attempted to employ some of the strategies of cultural inclusion with regard to language, the overall response from students was favorable. For example in one college communications course, I utilized the language of hip-hop slang, welcoming the students to class with "yo" or "what up" or "what's good?" as they introduced themselves on the first day of class. I continued to speak this way throughout the duration of the class which lasted just over one hour. At the next class meeting, I used a more formal or Standard version of English to lay the foundation for the direction of the course for the remainder of the semester and then explained that I code-switched not only to show that hip-hop language could in fact be spoken in a college classroom by a person in a position of some semblance of power. I asked the students what they thought about my language after the first day of class. Their selected responses were:

> I thought you was playin' or something 'cause I had a class with you before and you didn't sound like that.

I thought it was so cool and relaxed. I was so excited about the class.

I didn't think anything. I had never heard you speak before and just thought that was how you sounded. But, I didn't respect you any less. I thought you were smart.

I was telling my friends about it and I was like this class is going to be cool because the professor is real.

I was wondering if it was a joke or if you were trying to get us to relax since it was the first day.

The primary theme of the student responses was that hip-hop language used by me in my role as the instructor ran the gamut from being acceptable, welcome and strange to being a non-issue and a ruse. Pedagogy is an appropriate venue for both teacher and student to turn their consideration to the changing framework of education with language being used in this particular example. Of course, there will always be a divergence in the language we speak in the comfort of our own homes or in the presence of friends and family versus the language that we hear at a corporate meeting or classroom, but addressing these differences is a worthwhile lecture. The stories about language captured in this work offer some insight into the experiences of students. While these stories do not embody every student experience in every classroom, they are representative nonetheless of the empowerment that can be created with creative pedagogy.

The New York Times reports that over 55 million children will enroll in United States secondary schools in 2006, the largest number in American history. What's more, this class of students is also the most ethnically diverse. These students will look to their teachers for guidance and will merit the highest level of respect from those entrusted with their learning journey. No artificial barriers of inferiority, of which language is one should be welcome in any classroom.

In conclusion, I return to the story with which I began this chapter. That same year that I was in seventh grade and *Patchwork* was published, I learned a new word in English class. "Denouement" meant the "tying up of loose ends" in a story. After all of the pieces are put together, the story finishes with a sense of closure. At that time, our homework assignments frequently consisted of reading a story, noting all of the conflict in the story and then getting to the end of the story and ensuring that each conflict had been resolved. Seventh graders like myself at that time, endeavor for tidy endings wrapped up neat with a bow. For college professors and students, the journey to denouement is riddled with liberating stories that open up possibilities for healing, new directions in education and language freedom that are a long way from becoming neatly resolved. Yet, the telling of those stories themselves is denouement.

Bibliography

Allers, Kimberly L. "The new hustle: more rappers are moving from lyrics and videos to booming new business ventures. But too many have figured out the quickest route to riches." Essence, August 2005.

Andrews, William, L., Frances Smith Foster and Trudier Harris, The Oxford Companion to African-American Literature. New York: Oxford University Press, 1997.

Bell, Derrick. Gospel Choirs. New York: BasicBooks, 1996.

Blank, Renee and Sandra Slipp. Voices of Diversity: Real People Talk About Problems and Solutions in a Workplace Where Everyone is Not Alike. New York: Amacom.

Bourdieu, Pierre. On Television. New York: New Press, 1996.

Bourdieu, Pierre. Language and Symbolic Power. Cambridge: Harvard University Press, 1991.

Bragg, Melvyn. The Adventure of English: The Biography of a Language. New York: Arcade Publishing, 2003.

Braiker, Brian. California's Latest Sound: 'Hyphy': The newest hip-hop out of Northern California could put the Bay Area back on the national music scene. But does this post-'crunk' trend have staying power? Newsweek at MSNBC.com, January 14, 2005.

Burke, David. Without Slang and Idioms, Students are in the Dark! ESL Magazine at www.eslmag.com.

Byrne, Dan. Exalting 'ethnic' slang usage promotes racism to the highest degree. Echo-online, Wednesday, October 8, 2003 at www.easternecho.com.

Callahan-Bever, Noah. "The Last Laugh." Vibe Magazine. July 2005.

Clancy, John. The Invisible Powers: The Language of Business. New York: Lexington Books.

CNN Money. Iacocca Teams with Snoop Dogg. Reports: Chrysler aiming for younger car buyers, team retired chairman with rapper in new ad. August 2005. cnn.com.

Cooper, Thomas C. "Does it Suck?" or "Is it for the Birds?" Native Speaker Judgment of Slang Expression. American Speech, 2001 (pp. 62–78).

Daley, Mike. Black English and Rap Music: A Comparison. 14 May, 1998. York University.

DeBose, Charles. The Sociology of African American language. New York: Palgrave-McMillan, 2005.

Delpit, Lisa and Joanne Kilgour Dowdy. The Skin That We Speak: Thoughts on Language and Culture in the Classroom. New Press, 2002.

Dillon, Sam. In Schools Across U.S., the Melting Pot Overflows, The New York Times, Sunday, August 27, 2006; accessed at Newbank Inc.

Durham, Meenakshi Gigi and Douglas M. Kellner (eds), Media and Cultural Studies. Malden, Massachusetts: Blackwell Publishing, 2001.

Dyer, Leigh. Eastland Mall's identity in flux. The Charlotte Observer. June 10, 2006, page 2D.

Ebel, Connie C. Slang, Metaphor and Folk Speech, American Speech, Supplement Issue 88, 2003, page 157.

Fine, Marlene G. and Carolyn Anderson. Dialectical Features of Black Characters in Situation Comedies on Television. Phylon (1960), Vol 41, No. 4 (4th Qtr., 1980) pp. 396–409.

Ford, Bette "Talkin' Proper." American Quarterly—Volume 50, Number 1, March 1998, pp. 125–129.

Friere, Freire. Pedagogy of the Oppressed. New York: Continuum Books, 1993.

Gates, Henry Louis. Oxford Companion to Literature. 1997.

Giroux, Henry A., and Roger I. Simon. *Popular culture, schooling, and everyday life* Critical studies in education series. Granby, Mass.: Bergin & Garvey, 1989.Green, Maxine. Landscapes of Learning. New York: Teachers College Press, 1978.

Giroux, Henry A. *Doing Cultural Studies: Youth and the Challenge of Pedagogy*; Penn State University (accessed from the web).

Grossberg, Lawrence, Cary Nelson and Paula Treichler. *Cultural Studies*. New York: Routledge, 1992.

Guccione, Bob, Jr. "Planet Hip-hop." Gear Magazine, March 2002.

Hansen, David. *Exploring the Moral Heart of Teaching: Toward a Teacher's Creed*. New York: Teachers College Press, 2001. 240 pp.

Hooks, Bell. Teaching to Transgress: Education as the Practice of Freedom. New York: Routledge, 1995.

Howard, Theresa. "Rapper 50 Cent sings a song of business success" USA TODAY 7-4-2005.

Ismat, Abdal-Haqq. *Culturally Responsive Curriculum*. ERIC Digest, 1994.

Kearney, Kevin. "Rapper Kanye West on the cover of *Time*: Will rap music shed its "gangster" disguise? World Socialist Website. September 30, 2005. http://wsws.org/articles/2005/sep2005/kany-s 30.shtml

Kellner, Douglas. Media Culture. New York: Routledge, 1995.

Ladson-Billings, Gloria. *The Dreamkeepers: Successful Teachers of African-American Children*. Harvard Educational Review. San Francisco: Jossey-Bass, 1994.

Lelinwalla, Mark. *Jay-Z Gets Personal on New HP Commercial*. Vibe.com, June 15, 2006.

Lee, Margaret G. *Out of the Hood and Into the News: Borrowed Black Verbal Expressions in a Mainstream Newspaper*. American Speech, Winter, 1999. Volume 74, Issue 4.

Lin, Rong-Gong, II. *Teachers Urged to Use Rap to Bridge the Education Gap*. Los Angeles Times. Metro Section; Part B Page 4, May 7, 2006.

McCarthy, Michael. *Rappers sample athletes' turf.* USA TODAY, July 4, 2005.

Monahan, Julie. Chat Gets Serious: *Instant messaging presents service opportunities for banks, as well as some challenges, like keeping the chat productive.* Banking Strategies September/October 2003. Volume LXXIX Number V.

Moody, Nekesa Mumbi. *New Artists Breaking Musical Stereotypes.* Yahoo.music.com, December 17, 2003.

Moore, Robert L. "We're Cool, Mom and Dad are Swell: Basic Slang and Generational Shifts in Values. *American Speech,* 2004.

Neal, Mark Anthony. What the Music Said: Black Popular Music and Black Popular Culture. New York: Routledge, 1999.

Ogunnaike, Lola. "West World." Rolling Stone. February 6, 2006.

Pan, Tiffany. *Young UCLA scholars recognize the importance of studying hip-hop.* Daily Bruin via U-Wire, May 10, 2006.

Parker, Erik. "Hip-hop Goes Commercial: Rappers Give Madison Avenue a Run for Its Money." Village Voice. September 2002.

Pattillo-McCoy, Mary. Black Picket Fences: Privilege and Peril among the Black Middle Class. Chicago: University of Chicago Press, 1999.

Perry, Theresa. The Real Ebonics Debate. Boston: Beacon Press, 1998.

Rickford, John Russell and Russell John Rickford. Spoken Soul: The Story of Black English. New York: John Wiley & Sons, 2000.

Savan, Leslie. Slam Dunks and No-brainers: Language in your life, the media, business, politics, and like, whatever. New York: Alfred A. Knopf, 2005.

Sherr, Susan. News for a New Generation, Report One: Content Analysis, Interviews and Focus Groups, Page 4. Rutgers, The State University of New Jersey. Eagleton Institute of Politics.

Smitherman, Geneva. "The Chain Remains the Same: Communicative Practices in the Hip-hop Nation." Journal of Black Studies. September 1997.

Smitherman, Geneva. Talkin that Talk: Language, Culture and Education in African-America. New York: Routledge, 2000.

Spears, Richard A. *NTC's Dictionary of American Slang and Colloquial Expressions*. Chicago: Lincolnwood, 2000.

Spivey, Angela. Speaking in Tongues: http://research.unc.edu/endeavors/end1295/tongues.htm.

Tatum, Beverly Daniel. "Why are all the black kids sitting together in the cafeteria?" And other conversations about race. USA: BasicBooks, 1997.

The Museum of Broadcast Communications. http://www.museum.tv/archives/etv/G/htmlG/goodtimes/goodtimes.htm.

Tyrangiel, Josh. "Why you can't ignore Kanye West." Time, August 2005.

Valdez, Mimi from 'Hood goes Corporate, November 27, 2005, Los Angeles Times http://www.latimes.com/news/printedition/suncommentary/la-op-hiphopcommercial27nov27,1,133690.story?coll=la-headlines-suncomment.

Vlasic, Bill. *Chrysler pitchman proves he's still master of the deal*. The Detroit News, August 2005.

Wiehl, Lis. *Court-sanctioned Racial Stereotyping*, 18 Harvard BlackLetter Law Journal 185–210, 185–188 (Spring, 2002).

Yancy, George "Geneva Smitherman: The Social Ontology of AfricanAmerican Language, the Power of Nommo, and the Dynamics of Resistance and Identity Through Language." The Journal of Speculative Philosophy—Volume 18, Number 4, 2004 (New Series), pp. 273–299.

Index

academic, 15, 23, 29, 30, 74, 116, 119
Anderson, Carolyn, 81–83, 134
Baker, Houston. 77
Bell, Derrick, 97
black, 97, 98, 100, 102, 105–108, 116, 120, 122, 128, 134, 135, 136, 137
Black Vernacular English, 15, 96
Bogle, Donald, 13
Bourdieu, Pierre, 15, 133
Br'er Rabbit, 40, 69
Brinkley, David, 34, 70
Broadus, Calvin, 100, 102
Brown, Claude, 91
business, 8, 14, 21, 31, 46, 54, 57, 68, 70, 71, 82, 87, 91, 97, 98, 99, 101–106, 108–09, 113, 115, 117, 121, 133–136
Chancellor, John, 34, 70
children, 12, 13, 32, 34, 127, 130, 135
Chrysler, 100–13, 134, 137
church, 9. 21, 27, 48, 54, 67, 73–76, 92–93, 117, 126
code-switching, 70, 72–73, 85, 96, 119, 129, 131, 135
college, 20–24, 28, 30–32, 34, 36–37, 41–42, 44, 49–50, 63, 68–69, 72–73, 80, 87, 97, 111, 119–120
commercials, 44, 66, 99, 100, 102–105, 135–137

communication, 7, 79–81, 91, 108–109, 125, 127, 129, 137
conversation, 21, 25, 27, 37, 72, 88–89, 101, 125–126, 137
corporate, 104–106, 130
Cronkite, Walter, 34, 70
culture, 4, 14–15, 35, 68, 70, 72, 79, 88, 91–95, 97–98, 106, 108, 116–117, 119, 120–124, 126–129, 134–136
cultural studies, 128–129, 134–135
curriculum, 14, 119, 123, 127–128, 135
denouement, 130–131
dialogue, 56, 79, 116, 124
dominant, 79, 93–94, 96–98, 119
Dyson, Michael Eric, 92, 116
Ebonics, 77, 136
English, 4, 11, 13–15, 19–20, 22–23, 31–32, 34–36, 46, 50, 52, 55, 58, 62–63, 66, 69–74, 76–77, 81–82, 85, 87–88, 91–92, 96, 103, 105, 110–111, 113, 116–117, 122, 125–130, 133–136
fantasy, 85, 87, 89
fashion, 85, 91, 97, 100, 104
Fine, Marlene G., 81–83, 134
Fiske, John, 79
Ford, Bette, 73
Freire, Paulo, 123, 134
Fresh Prince of Bel-Air, 5, 13, 83–87
Gates, Henry Louis, 69, 93–95, 134

Index

ghetto, 87–88, 96, 108
Giroux, Henry, 128
Good Times, 5, 13–14, 80, 82–85, 87
Grand Ole Opry, 89
Greene, Maxine, 123, 135
Hewlett–Packard, 103–104
hillbilly, 11
hip-hop, 5, 14, 84–85, 90–111, 116–117, 119, 121–122, 125–127, 129–130, 135–136
hood, 13, 104, 135, 137
Iacocca, Lee, 100–102, 134
Internet, 106, 108
Jay-Z, 5, 92–96, 98–99, 103, 135
Jones, Tom, 13
Kellner, Douglas, 92–96, 98, 135
Ladson-Billings, Gloria, 124, 135
language, 4–5, 7–9, 11, 14–15, 19–77, 79–131, 133–134, 136–137
linguistic capital, 14
linguistics, 11, 19
McDonalds, 104
McRobbie, Angela, 119–120
media, 14, 23, 63–64, 73, 87, 93, 95, 108, 115, 120, 123–124, 129, 134–136
message, 63, 85, 105, 108–110, 127
metaphor, 82, 106, 134
multicultural, 124–125
Museum of Broadcast Communications, 79–81, 137
music, 13–14, 23, 53, 61–62, 69, 72, 77, 88, 90–94, 96–100, 103–106, 108, 113, 115–117, 119, 127, 133–136
Neal, Mark Anthony, 91–92, 136
nerd, 13
New York Times, 130, 134
Nike, 100, 104
pedagogy, 14, 69, 119, 128, 130, 134–135

popular culture, 14, 79, 117, 119–120, 124, 126–127, 135–136
rap music, 113–116, 119, 134–135
representation, 14–15, 70, 95, 119–120, 124, 126–127, 135–136
Ribeira, Alphonso, 13
Rolling Stone, 99, 136
school, 12–13, 23–25, 28–30, 32, 35, 50, 52, 63, 66, 73, 75–76, 81, 83–85, 89, 92, 97, 106, 111, 113–115, 117, 120–122, 124–127, 130, 134–135
signifyin', 69, 93–95, 97–99
slang, 5, 13, 84–85, 87, 92, 96, 99, 102, 105–106, 108–109, 112–115, 117, 119–122, 125, 129, 133–134, 136
Smith, Will, 13–14, 83–84
Smitherman, Geneva, 70, 74, 91, 125, 136–137
Snoop Dogg, 100–103, 112, 116, 134
song, 55, 61–62, 75, 84, 88, 92–95, 97–100, 103, 105, 112, 114, 116, 135
southern, 11, 30, 34, 39, 65, 70, 76, 96, 108
Stone, Joss, 108
survival, 98, 116
teacher, 38, 50, 67, 73, 75, 84–85, 106, 113, 117, 119, 123–124, 127–128, 130, 135,
television, 5, 7–8, 11, 13–14, 22, 34–35, 64, 69, 79, 80–90, 93, 99–100, 112, 117, 133–134
triangulation, 124
Vittles, 11
Walker, Jimmie, 13, 80
West, Kanye, 93–94, 96–99, 135, 137
white, 7, 12–13, 23–24, 32, 34, 45, 66, 69, 70–72, 74–75, 77,

79–80, 83–85, 87–89, 92–93, 98, 102–103, 105–108
worship, 93

York Comprehensive High School, 111, 114–115